MW00748554

A JOURNEY THROUGH

CHINA

Exploring Major Sites and
Cuisine in 10 Days

The Reader's Digest Association, Inc.
Pleasantville, New York / Montreal / Sydney

Content

Stop 4: Hangzhou

Stop 5: Guilin

Stop 6: Hong Kong

Appendix

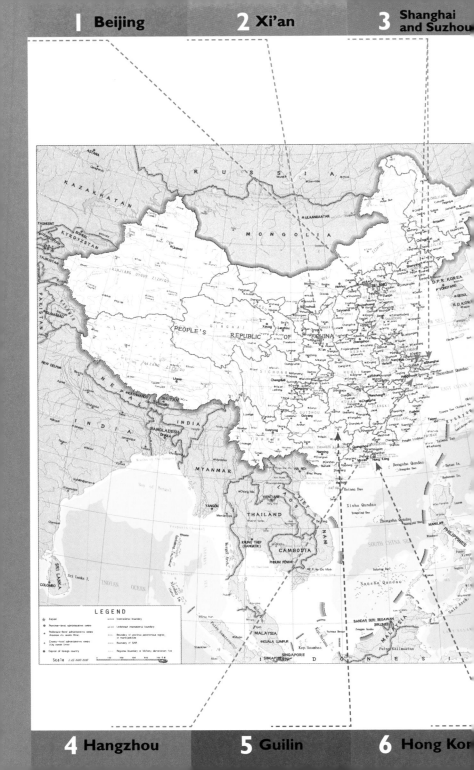

Introduction

If you have only ten days to spend in China, what places should you not miss? Although it is impossible to travel all around this large territory in a few days, you can still go to some representative cities to experience China's unique landscape, culture, history, and the dynamic rhythm of its development.

The seven places recommended in this book scatter in different regions of China. They possess distinguished features and praise from tourist for beauty achieved both by nature and historical changes spanning over thousand years, and diversified unique cuisines. Immerse yourself in China's rich history in imperial Beijing and its ancient capital of Xi'an. In contrast, take in the energetic and progressive cities of Hong Kong and Shanghai to experience modern China. To take a break from the action, relax in the picturesque settings of Suzhou and Hangzhou, Which have both been called "heaven on earth." In Guilin, you'll find breathtaking landscapes praised as the best in country.

As Shanghai and Suzhou are adjacent to each other, they are arranged together in one stop. Each section contains highlights meant to suit a variety of interests. Visitors will find cultural and historic sights, shopping and entertainment, and spectacular city and natural landscapes while traveling in China. This journey of six coherent, but distinctive stops will show you the diversified beauty of China, and help you experience Chinese food from all over the country in different kinds of restaurants—from the exquisite dishes fit for loyalty to the simplest, most delicious of snacks.

Stop 1: Beijing

Beijing

Must-go Places Introduction

General Information

Beijing, also called Jing for short, is the capital of the People's Republic of China. It is a municipality directly under the central government that is opening up to the outside world. With 16 districts and 2 counties under its administrative jurisdiction, Beijing has a total area of 16,800 sq. km and a population of 16 million, with the ethnic groups of the Han, Man, Hui, and Mongol.

Environment

Beijing is located at the northwest end of the North China Plain. It is surrounded by Hebei Province, except for the eastern and southeastern corners, which are bordered with Tianjin Municipality. Its terrain is descending from the northwest to southeast. It has a typical semi-humid warm continental monsoon climate, with an average temperature of -10~-5°C in January and 22~26°C in July, and an average annual rainfall between 500~700 mm.

Places of Interest

Beijing is one of the seven major ancient cities in China, boasting a history of more than 3000 years. The Peking Man, found in Zhoukoudian and dating back to 500,000 years ago, is the earliest origin of the ethnic groups in the Central Plains. Kublai Khan of the Yuan dynasty (1279–1368) constructed fortresses and dug canals to establish the Grand Capital here. The May 4 Movement (an anti-imperialist, cultural, and political movement on 1919) and the founding of New China opened a new chapter in the history and culture of the city.

Beijing has the largest number of cultural sites in China. Among them are the towering Great Wall, the glittering and splendid Imperial Palace, the vast Ming Tombs, the magnificent Temple of Heaven, Beihai Park, the Summer Palace, as well as the Zhoukoudian site of the Peking Man, the internationally renowned Lugou Bridge (Marco Polo Bridge), and the Ancient Observatory. Religious places of interest are the Biyun Temple, the Baiyun Taoist Temple, the Yonghe Lamasery and the Niujie Mosque that all have a long history of cultural significance. The alleys and quadrangle courtyards in Beijing reflect the strong style of old city.

The fame of the natural scenic spots of Beijing are carried far and wide. There are the Xiangshan Hills (Fragrant Hills) normally covered with the red leaves of maple trees in the fall, Zizhu (Purple Bamboo) Garden with exuberant bamboo woods, Yuyuantan Park with an elegant and quiet environment, Shidu Gorge in the suburbs of Beijing, Miaofeng Mountain, Longqing Gorge, and Yougu Shentan (Secluded Dell and Immortal's Pond).

The Great Wall
chang cheng
长城

Nothing can really compare to the immense human labor that went into the construction and almost constant renovation and expansion of the greatest monument to Chinese civilization: the Great Wall.

Initiated during the Qin dynasty (221 BC–206 BC) in the 3rd century BC, when the emperor ordered the linking up of older tribal walls, the Great Wall forced into labor some 500,000 peasants, among them many convicted criminals. In the later interim and unstable rule of the Northern Wei (AD 386–AD 534), another 300,000 people were put to work on a single section south of Datong. In AD 607–AD 608, when north-south political divisions were still shaking the foundations of Chinese unity, a full 1 million people were further called upon. But all this paled against the many millions of laborers conscripted during the Ming dynasty (1368–1644) to modernize, strengthen and extend the wall—this stage of the project alone took more than 100 years to complete.

The result is nothing short of a human marvel, a man-made protective barrier that snakes a distance of 3728 mi. (6000 km) over and through the rumpled folds of the northern Chinese landscape from Shanhaiguan Pass on the shores of the Bo Sea, through Hebei, Shanxi, Inner Mongolia, Shaanxi, Ningxia and Gansu provinces until it reaches Jiayuguan in the arid west. It is a monument to the human spirit and a memorial to immense human suffering. During each work campaign, thousand died of sickness, accident, exposure or simply the physical ordeal. Almost everything was done by hand, passing from one to another the raw materials

—rock, earth, bricks, lime and site. Handcarts were used on flat land or gentle slopes, and goats and donkeys sometimes hauled the bricks and lime, but otherwise it was harsh and unremitting human toil that built this most spectacular man-made structure.

The Great Wall of the Warring States Period

Long before the Great Wall itself was built, primitive defensive mounds and walls were thrown up here and there throughout northern China to protect tribal groups from surprise attack. According to ancient records, the state of Chu built walls in the 7th century BC in the areas that are now Henan and Hubei provinces.

The Great Wall of the Warring States emerged from several defensive lines of tamped earth built by the various states, and it was these unconnected walls that were joined together and strengthened to form the first stage of the Great Wall in the Qin dynasty. The Qi wall was built

in the 5th century BC in what is now the province of Shandong. It runs from Pingyin in the west, around the northern slopes of Tai Mountain, and ends at the coast.

Watchtowers of the Great Wall
(长城烽火台 *chang cheng feng huo tai*)

There were two types of watchtowers built along the Great Wall —*qiang tai* (wall towers), which were erected on the wall itself or jutted from its sides, and *di tai* (enemy towers), which were two-story fortifications containing living quarters and arsenals and crenellated parapets. Many of these enemy towers can still be found along a 311 mi. (500 km) section of relatively intact wall in the northern part of Hebei Province. Designed by the Ming general Qi Jiguang, they were placed at short intervals, particularly between Juyongguan Pass and Shanhaiguan Pass.

Jinshanling Wall
(金山岭长城 *jin shan ling chang cheng*)

One particularly well-defended stretch of the wall—now crumbling

in many places—was built in 1570 by General Qi Jiguang to cover a series of low rolling hills at Jinshanling. Because the open, gently rising terrain gave any enemy easy access to the Han hinterland, the wall along this 19-mi. (30-km) section was heavily strengthened and well fortified with watchtowers and beacon posts.

Admission:
🕐 5:00~17:00 (Apr. 1~Oct. 31)
¥ 50
🕐 7:00~17:00 (Nov.1~Mar. 31)
¥ 40
📞 0314-8830555

Juyongguan Pass
(居庸关 *ju yong guan*)

When the first emperor of Qin completed the first stage of the Great Wall's construction, he found he had another problem on his hands—many hundreds of unwanted laborers. He resettles them at Juyongguan Pass in Changping County of what is now Beijing—the name Juyong believed to be a shortened version of Xi Ju Yong Tu, meaning "to resettle redundant people."

But Juyongguan Pass has an important strategic place in history too. Flanked by high mountains and straddling a 12-mi.-long (20-km-long) gully, it was regarded as a vital linchpin in the defense of northern China and apparently so indomitable that it was the subject of at least one poetic tribute: "With only one soldier to defend the place, even ten thousand attackers will fail to capture it."

Near Juyongguan Pass there is a platform called Yun Tai (Cloud Platform) built in 1345 of white marble. It once supported three Buddhist stupas, which were destroyed around the time of the late Yuan dynasty. A nearby monastery, Taian, built in 1439, was burned down in 1702. What is left of Yun Tai, the base, features an arched gate 23 ft (7 m) high and wide enough for

a carriage to be driven through. The facade is decorated with Buddhist images which were carved there during the Ming reign.

Admission:
🕐 7:30~17:00 (Apr. 1~Oct. 31)
¥ 40
🕐 8:30~16:30 (Nov.1~Mar. 31)
¥ 35
✆ 010-69771665

Badaling Wall
(八达岭长城 *ba da ling chang cheng*)

The Badaling (Eight-Reaching Pass) section of the Great Wall climbs high up a mountain range in the Yanqing County of Beijing and offers one of the best surviving examples of the Wall's defensive architecture and fortification. This area of the Wall and its garrison were built in 1505 in the reign of the Ming emperor, Xiaozong, and they were definitely built to last. The wall itself is higher than most other sections, rests on huge stone slabs and is constructed almost entirely of brick and stone. The parapets are crenellated, and the lower sections of the walls have loopholes for defensive fire by arches. The top surface of the wall is 16 ft (5 m) wide, with space enough for 5 horses of 10 soldiers to march abreast along it.

Admission:
🕐 6:30~18:00 (Apr. 1~Oct. 31)
¥ 45
🕐 7:00~17:00 (Nov.1~Mar. 31)
¥ 40
✆ 010-69121226
@ www.badaling.gov.cn

The Forbidden City
gu gong
故宫

Better known all over the world as Beijing's Forbidden City, the Ancient Palaces were the residence and political nerve center of the emperors of the Ming and succeeding Qing dynasties, and the hotbed of intrigue among their huge courts. The original palaces, which took 15 years to build, were started in 1406 by the third emperor of the Ming dynasty, Chengzu, when he moved the imperial capital to Beijing. The complex, the largest surviving cluster of wooden buildings on such a scale in the world, has since played a central role in the most momentous phases of contemporary Chinese history—the wealth, power and glory of the Ming, the Manchu triumph of the Qing dynasty (1644–1911), then its gradual decay in the face of foreign pressure and incursion, and finally the complete collapse of the dynastic order. After the fall of the Qing and establishment of the short-lived Chinese republic, the Forbidden City fell into disrepair but was restored in the 1950s according to its original plans—the spirits of 24 great and not-so-great divine rulers of China's immense past still facing south, according to ancient Chinese geomancy, and their people facing north in obeisance.

The Forbidden City is girdled by a 10-m-high city wall and a 52-m-wide moat. It measures 961m long from north to south and 753 m wide from east to west, covering 780,000 sq.m. There is a gate on each side of the rectangular city wall. The layout of the architecture's complex within the city

all centers on the north-south axis and sprawls eastward and westward. The architecture's red walls, golden glazed tiles, engraved beams, painted rafters rival in magnificence.

The Palace Museum was founded in 1925 to oversee the protection of the existing relics and artifacts in the collections of the Forbidden City.

Wu Men
(午门 *wu men*)

The gigantic terrace, on which stand the Five Phoenix Mansions, is the main front entrance to the Forbidden City. Wu Men (Meridian Gate) is where the emperors issued edicts, had miscreant mandarins publicly flogged and presided over the execution of common criminals sharp

at noon. Built in 1420 and rebuilt in 1647, it is actually five gateways, the central one reserved for the emperor's carriages. Once inside, visitors and emissaries proceeded to the Hall of Supreme Harmony (Taihe Dian), where the rulers conducted state ceremonies and political business, or to the Hall of Preserving Harmony (Baohe Dian), which was the setting for state banquets and, at one time, the examination hall for civil service candidates. Another mansion, Hall of Central Harmony (Zhonghe Dian), was where the emperors studied briefing papers before attending meetings in the Taihe Hall. An inner section of the palaces, north of Baohe Hall, included the emperor's living quarters and Imperial Garden.

Corner Pavilion
(角楼 *jiao lou*)

The Forbidden City was so called because the common people were forbidden to enter it, and observation and security towers placed at each corner of the 1.6-million-sq. ft (150,000-sq.-m) palace grounds made certain that all but the aristocracy were kept out. These pavilions were based

on the designs of the Yellow Crane and Prince Teng mansions of the Song dynasty (AD 960–1279), and today their complex and extravagant roof structures are regarded as yet another masterpiece of traditional architecture.

Qianqing Hall
(乾清殿 *qian qing dian*)

This Qing dynasty reception and banqueting hall also served a crucial role in the security and harmony of the dynastic order. It was where the Qing emperors chose their successors. From the time of Emperor Yongzheng, who assumed the throne in 1723, it was the custom for each ruler to write the name of his intended successor on two pieces of paper—one to be kept in his personal possession and

the other secreted behind a plaque bearing the inscription "Frank and Honest." Upon the emperor's death, his closest minister would compare the two names, and if they tallied, they announced the new ruler. More than 40 mansions surround the Qianqing Hall, some of them containing the emperor's crown and robes of office and books and artworks; other being places where he held audiences with his chief scholars and advisers; and still others being used as reading rooms, medical consulting rooms and living quarters for the imperial servants, maids, concubines and palace eunuchs.

Admission:
🕐 8:30~17:00 (Apr. 1~Oct. 31), Last Entry at 16:10
¥ 60
🕐 8:30~16:30 (Nov.1~Mar. 31), Last Entry at 15:40 (Including the Clock Gallery and Treasure Gallery)
¥ 40
Treasure Gallery and Clock Gallery Require A Separate Ticket
¥ 10 Respectively
📞 010-65132255
@ www.dpm.org.cn

The Summer Palace
yi he yuan
颐和园

The powerful and ruthless Empress Dowager (Cixi), the last real dynastic ruler of China, built the Summer Palace in 1888 on the site of a previous palace and garden that had dated from the Jin dynasty (1115–1234). The project has since been regarded as something of an extravagant folly. For one thing, the empress appropriated much of the cost of it, some 24 million taels of silver, from funds set up to modernize the Chinese navy—and was soon to see the navy, or fleets of magnificent but obsolete and outgunned war junks, suffer a humiliating defeat under the guns and rockets of British iron-hulled steam-paddle warship brought from England to smash open the doors to free trade in China. As for the Summer Palace itself, Allied Forces gutted and plundered it two years after it had been completed, and a subsequent rebuilding project only added to its vast cost. Nowadays its lake, gardens, shrines and pavilions are open to the public, along with another symbol of the Empress Dowager's stubborn extravagance, the giant Marble Boat on Kunming Lake, a stone replica of a showboat paddle steamer.

A bronze pavilion, called Pavilion of Precious Clouds, is another feature

of the Summer Palace. It was cast in 1750 and reaches a height of nearly 26 ft (8 m) and weighs more than 200 tons.

The Long Gallery
(长廊 *chang lang*)

This corridor, 2400 ft (728 m) long, follows the line of the northern bank of Kunming Lake and is designed to reflect its special blend of architecture and nature in the still waters around it. Its ceiling is also painted with some 8000 "still life" compositions of flowers and scenes from famous Chinese stories and legends, and for this reason it is also called the Picture Corridor. Halfway along the gallery lies the Empress Dowager's opulent Palace Which Dispels Clouds; further along stands the beautiful Listening to Orioles Hall (Tingliguan); and at the end of the corridor the garish white Marble Boat reflects the sudden twist of

refinement to vulgarity that took place in the Empress Dowager's reign.

Kunming Lake
(昆明湖 *kun ming hu*)

A number of streams from the western districts of Beijing, including one called Jade Spring Mountain, were channeled by engineers of the Yuan dynasty to form the great lake of the Summer Palace. The Qing emperor, Qianlong, gave it its name when he refurbished a Ming dynasty palace and temple, the Duobao Pagoda, to celebrate his mother's 60th birthday. Later, the Empress Dowager added much of the rest of the construction around the lake, including the Palace Which Dispels Clouds, which she built to celebrate her own birthday.

Admission:
- Gate: 6:30~18:00 (Apr. 1~Oct. 31) Parks Inside the Summer Palace: 8:30~17:00, Close: 20:00
- ¥ 60
- Gate: 7:00~17:00 (Nov. 1~Mar.31) Parks Inside the Summer Palace: 9:00~16:00, Close: 19:00
- ¥ 50
- 010-62881144
- @ www.summerpalace-china.com

Temple of Heaven

tian tan

天坛

Tiantan, the Temple of Heaven, in the southwestern corner of Beijing, is an ensemble of shines and was once the venue for the most important imperial rite—prayers for good harvest, sacrifices to the gods and royal ancestors and communion with the heavens. Built in 1420 (the 18th year of the reign of the Ming emperor Yongle), the building is part of a series of four temples in Beijing representing the firmament, the others being the Temple of the Sun, the Temple of the Earth and the Temple of the Moon. The buildings are spaced out over an area of more than 29.4 million sq. ft (2,700,000 sq. m), and altogether took 14 years to build.

The Temple of Heaven consists of two main structures linked by an 1188-ft-long (360-m-long) bridge. It is regarded as the most remarkable architectural composition, in which mathematical balance and economy of design have achieved an almost overwhelming majesty. It is also a masterpiece of acoustics, its most novel feature being a circular wall of polished bricks in Huangqiong House (Imperial Vault of Heaven), where echoes run clearly from one end to another, giving it the name Echo Wall.

Admission:
🕐 The Park: 6:00~22:00
🕐 Major Sightseeing Spots:
    8:00~17:30 (Mar.1~Jun.30)
    8:00~18:00 (Jul.1~Oct.31)
    8:00~17:00 (Nov.1~Feb.28)
¥ 35 (Apr.1~Oct. 31)
¥ 30 (Nov.1~Mar. 31)
☎ 010-67028866
@ www.tiantanpark.com

This hall also contains sacred ancestral tablets, as well as those dedicated to the gods of rain, the sun, the moon, the stars, dawn, wind, thunder and lightning. When Western troops invaded Beijing in 1860 and 1900, the Temple of Heaven suffered serious damage, and it was not until 1918 that the temple was repaired and reopened to the public.

Qiniandian
（祈年殿 *qi nian dian*）

The Temple for Praying for a Good Harvest with a detail of its domed ceiling, dominates the Temple of Heaven from the top of three concentric terraces fenced with carved white marble balustrades. It is where the emperor came each year at the first full moon for fertility rites that go back to the distant beginnings of Chinese history. At the winter solstice he would also mount the three terraces of the Circular Sacrificial Altar where, after much prayer and traditional clay pipe music, a young bullock would be sacrificed to the gods. As such, the emperor was the vital conduit between the teeming Chinese society and the spiritual forces that ruled much of its existence. Though sometimes a harsh and despotic ruler himself, he was also servant of two masters—acting as vehicle through which the people's fears and wishes were made known to the heavenly deities, and a kind of human lightning rod for bolts of good fortune or retribution from on high.

Beihai (North Sea) Park
bei hai gong yuan
北海公园

For more than 1000 years the Beihai Park—as mundane as its name may be—was the royal garden of successive dynasties that included the Liao (AD 916–1125), Jin (1125–1234), Yuan and Ming. It covers an area of 7.6 million sq. ft (700,000 sq. m), and among its beautifully landscaped gardens, hillocks and pools there are two particular artistic attractions. One, the famous Nine Dragon Wall, is an 86-ft-long (26-m-long) ceramic monument made up of 424 seven-colored glazed tiles depicting nine dragons in high relief on each side. The other showpiece is the White Stupa (or Dagoba), which is a prime example of Tibetan Buddhist architecture. Built in 1651, it was badly damaged by earthquakes in 1679 and 1731.

Quiet Mind Studio of Qianlong
(静心斋 *jing xin zhai*)

Nature and the architect's vision have blended splendidly to create this garden within a garden, originally called Jingxinzhai, or Quiet Mind Studio, on the northern shore of Beihai in Beijing. It features elaborate formations of rocks from Lake Tai in artificial hills and craggy shorelines around the garden's lotus and lily covered ponds, and a series of peaceful pavilions and water bowers. Constructed in 1758, Quiet Mind Studio was completely renovated in 1913 after the fall of the dynastic order and was used as a reception venue for foreign diplomats.

Admission:
🕓 6:00~21:00 (April, May, September, and October)
🕓 6:00~22:00 (June, July, and August)
🕓 6:30~20:00 (January, February, March, November and December)
¥ 10 (Apr.1~Oct.31)
¥ 5 (Nov.1~Mar. 31)
✆ 010-64033225
@ www.beihaipark.com.cn

Yuanmingyuan Park
yuan ming yuan
圆明园

The ruins of Yuanmingyuan Park, the imperial gardens of the Summer Palace outside Beijing, are still a famous destination in China even though few traces of its magnificent beauty remain today. In the past, the gardens were the home of the emperor and his court from the beginning of each Chinese lunar New Year in early spring until autumn. For over 150 years the gardens, bridges, pagodas and residences were the pet project of emperors who based their design on well-known scenic spots in China and other famous garden designs. The area for the gardens was already blessed with an abundance of natural springs and hills, but that was just the raw material for the creation of a fairytale landscape that exemplified the imperial desire to have all the beauty of China belong within the emperor's garden walls. Rivers, waterfalls, lakes and islands dotted the transformed landscape. The theme of each special garden site was created to represent China's cherished artistic, literary and philosophical concepts that the emperor then had the privilege of naming. The finest materials went in to the building of

the garden's exquisite architecture. These marvelous structures were furnished from the vast imperial collections of art, antiques and books. As contact with the west began to influence imperial taste, western building and art objects were added to Yuanmingyuan Park. The gardens represented the culmination of 2000 years of Chinese garden design. Sadly, the weakened Qing dynasty in the second half of the 19th century was unable to protect China, and as foreign powers vied in Beijing for the rich spoils, the imperial gardens were eventually set on fire and the treasures looted. For many years, even after being in a disastrous state of ruin, the gardens inspired poetry describing its tragic beauty.

Admission:
🕐 7:00~18:00 (April, September, and October)
🕐 7:00~19:00 (May, June, July, and August)
🕐 7:00~17:30 (January, February, March, November and December)
¥ 10
✆ 010-62637561
    010-62628501

Yonghe Lamasery
yong he gong
雍和宫

The Qing emperor Yongzheng lived in this complex first as a prince and later as emperor, using parts of the premises for the practice of Tibetan Buddhism. When the emperor died, his coffin was lodged here, and the green roof tiles were replaced by yellow ones, whereby the place was officially elevated to the rank of a palace for housing Yongzheng's image and for the ancestral worship of the royal Qing house. The palace was presented to the lamas by Emperor Qianlong in 1744 and turned into a lamasery, and it stands today as the largest and one of the best-preserved Buddhist institutions in China. In the five halls that make up the monastery, valuable Buddhist images in bronze and stone stand alongside rare relics of the Yellow Sect of Tibetan Buddhism, including ancient copies of the Tripitaka sutras. Its walls contain many colorful murals of Buddhist stories and Buddha images. The many side rooms also house valuable collections of Buddhist scriptures and writings in mathematics, medicine, astronomy, and geography.

Admission:
✆ 010-64044499

Fragrant Hills Park
xiang shan gong yuan
香山公园

This scenic park west of Beijing is a location that has been favored by imperial dynasties since the 12th century when it was chosen as an imperial hunting ground. Pavilions, temples and summer retreats for the imperial family have graced the park, but time, changes in fashion and the destruction of much imperial property in the late 19th century by foreign powers have conspired to remove many of the structures built in the park over its long history. The brilliant autumn foliage of the smoke trees that cover the hills to the west of the park has long made the park a popular destination. For the hardy admirers of nature, winter also is a favorite time to take in the beauty of snow-covered hills.

There are a number of temples in the park, including the Temple of Brilliance, a copy of a Tibetan temple. The delightful Glazed Tile Pagoda has bronze bells that tinkle in the wind

and hang from the eaves of each of its seven stories. A small garden within the park was once the site of the Summer Palace. The semicircular pool surrounded by a covered walkway is similar to the original that once decorated the grounds of the Summer Palace.

Glazed Pagoda of Fragrant Hills
(多宝琉璃塔 *duo bao liu li ta*)

This beautiful green pagoda is eight-sided and seven-tiered but only 33 ft (10 m) tall. It stands in Fragrant Hills Park in Beijing and was built in typical Qing dynasty fashion, with a combination of stone tiles and wooden corridors and 56 bronze wind bells tinkling from its many eaves. It is the only structure to survive inside the Zhao Temple, which was built in 1780 (the 45th year of the reign of the Qing emperor Qianlong) in the Tibetan style of architecture, and served as a guesthouse to the 6th Panchen lama when he visited Beijing. The pagoda, which lies to the west of it, is now regarded as the emblem of this complex.

Shifangpujue Monastery
(卧佛寺 *wo fo si*)

Located on the southern slope of Shou'an Hill just outside Beijing, this monastery was first built in the Tang dynasty (AD 618–AD 907) in the 7th century and rebuilt in 1734 (the 12th year of the Qing emperor Yongzheng). It is also called the Sleeping Buddha Monastery, because it houses a reclining statue of Buddha. The main feature of this symmetrically designed monastery is the Hall of the Sleeping Buddha, where a bronze image of Sakyamuni lies in an apparent state of Nirvana. The statue, cast in 1321 in the Yuan dynasty, is more than 17 ft (5 m) long and depicts Sakyamuni speaking with his disciples about his impending departure from all earthly things. Lying on one side, with his right hand pitched against his head, the Buddha is the very picture of ease and calm, attended by disciples represented here as 12 clay statues standing behind him.

Biyun Monastery
(碧云寺 *bi yun si*)

When Buddha first took root in China, its architecture naturally followed the style of that of its birthplace, India. But almost all early Chinese construction was of wood, and the evidence of whole periods of history was destroyed by fire. Through a combination of reconstruction and its own artistic development, Han Chinese architecture soon dominated the design of religious and public buildings. A group of white marble pagodas remains, however, as a striking example of early Indian design in the Biyun Monastery on the eastern slope of Fragrant Hills or Xiangshan, in Beijing. The tallest is 13-tiered and 116 ft (35 m) high and is decorated with Tibetan Buddhist themes in bas-relief.

Admission:
- 🕐 6:00~18:30 (Apr.1~Jun.30)
- 🕐 6:00~19:00 (Jul.1~Aug.31)
- 🕐 6:00~18:00 (Nov.16~Mar.31)
- ¥ 10 (Apr.1~Nov.15)
- ¥ 5 (Nov.16~Mar.31)
- ¥ 10 (Biyun Monastery)
- ✆ 010-62591264

Ming Tombs
ming shi san ling

明十三陵

Ranking with the Forbidden City and the Great Wall as one of the most renowned monuments to Chinese imperial history, the Ming tombs lie in the shadow of Tianshou Mountain 31 mi. (50 m) north of Beijing. They were built as mausoleums for 13 emperors of the Ming dynasty from reign of Chengzu to Sizong, covering a period of more than 200 years from 1409 to 1644. The approach to the tombs alone is monumental—an 11-story white marble memorial archway with five gates and six pillars is the main entrance; beyond it stands the Dahong Gate (Great Red Gate) with red walls and yellow roof tiles; and beyond that lies a wide 4-mi (7-km) Road of the Gods lined with large stone sculptures of lions, camels, elephants, unicorns and horses and statues of court officials in the ceremonial dress, each slightly bowed in a gesture of respect. The tombs of the emperors and their consorts are found in the Baocheng (Precious) City, each surrounded by a red wall and each containing a particular stone tablet that, unlike the others, has nothing inscribed upon it —symbolizing the infinite beneficence of the imperial rulers.

Chang Tomb
(长陵 *chang ling*)

No other tomb ranks in size and grandeur with the Chang Tomb, built in 1409 for the emperor Yongle. Its Lingen Hall stands on a 10-ft-(3-m-) high white marble podium. It covers an area of 20,452 sq. ft (1900 sq. m) and is supported by 60 timber columns that, five centuries later, are every bit as sturdy and well preserved as when they were first installed.

Chang Tomb is the first mausoleum to have been built, and it set the standard of design for the 12 other tombs that followed.

Ding Tomb
(定陵 *ding ling*)

Lying southwest of Chang Tomb below the Dayu Hill, Ding Tomb was built for Emperor Shenzong and his two queens. Started in 1548 when he was still alive, it was completed six years later. It features the Brilliant Tower, roofed with yellow-glazed cylindrical tiles and stone tablets inscribed with the words *da ming* (Great Ming) and Tomb of Shenzong, but otherwise there is little surface evidence of the far grander spectacle that lies under the ground behind this mausoleum entrance.

The Underground Palace
(地宫 *di gong*)

Right behind the Brilliant Tower of Ding Tomb lies the Underground Palace, or burial tomb, of Emperor Shenzong and his two queens, the only burial hall excavated so far in the Ming Tombs. Archeologists broke through to it in 1956 and found five chambers, each separated by a 4-ton stone door, that were as majestic as any of the Pharaonic tombs unearthed in Egypt.

Under the vast domed ceiling of the stone hall they found the coffins of Shenzong and his wives, along with golden crowns the other ceremonial headwear, porcelain, utensils, jade vases, silk wear and other burial possessions—the stone funerary bed lying in surroundings of bare simplicity

compared with the décor and furnishings of the adjoining chambers. There, the floors are paved with "gold" tiles impregnated with tung oil to give them a lasting luster, and the central chamber features intricately carved white marble benches, blue porcelain urns with dragon motifs and other Ming dynasty artwork.

Admission:
Ding Tomb:
🕐 8:00~17:30 (Apr.1~Oct.31)
🕐 8:30~17:00 (Nov.1~Mar.31)
¥ 40 (Nov. 1~Mar.31)
¥ 60 (Apr. 1~Oct.31)
✆ 010-60761424
ChangTomb:
🕐 8:00~17:00 (Apr.1~Oct.31)
🕐 8:30~16:30 (Nov.1~Mar.31)
¥ 30 (Nov. 1~Mar.31),
¥ 45 (Apr. 1~Oct. 31)
✆ 010-60761888
Zhao Tomb:
🕐 8:00~17:30 (Apr.1~Oct.31)
🕐 8:30~17:00 (Nov.1~Mar.31)
¥ 20 (Nov. 1~Mar.31)
¥ 30 (Apr. 1~Oct. 31)
✆ 010-60763104
Sacred Way:
🕐 8:00~17:30 (Apr.1~Oct.31)
🕐 8:30~16:30 (Nov.1~Mar.31)
¥ 20 (Nov. 1~Mar.31)
  30 (Apr. 1~Oct. 31)
✆ 010-89749383
@ www.mingtombs.com

Qing-Dongling
(Eastern Tombs of the Qing Emperors)
qing dong ling
清东陵

The Qing dynasty buried its emperors on a series of sites, the earliest of them in Zunhua County, 78 mi. (125 km) east of Beijing, named Dongling—a cluster of mausoleums that developed into the most extensive burial spot in China. The tombs were commenced in 1663, and emperors Shunzhi, Kangxi, Qianlong, Xianfeng and Tongzhi, along with their consorts and more that 100 concubines were laid to rest. Though not as ornate as the preceding Ming dynasty tombs, these burial places followed basically the same pattern of Great Red Gate entrances opening on to sacred avenues—a 3.7-mi. (6-km) approach in this case—lined with stone sculptures of animals and statues of civil and military officers.

Yu Mausoleum
(裕陵 *yu ling*)

The largest of the Qing-Dongling is that of Emperor Shunzhi, but the most impressive are those of Qianlong (Yu Mausoleum) and the Emperess Dowager Cixi. The underground palace of Yu Mausoleum is composed of nine arches and four gates totaling 54 m in length starting from the first stone gate, all the walls and arches are carved with Buddhist topics. The carvings, exquisite and smooth, are vivid to life and carefully patterned.

Admission:
🕐 8:00~17:00 (Apr. 1~Oct. 31)
🕐 8:30~16:30 (Nov. 1~Mar.31)
¥ 120/Adult
¥ 60/Student
✆ 0315-6940888
　 0315-6945475

Qing-Xiling
(Western Tombs of the Qing Emperors)
qing xi ling
清西陵

The other Qing dynasty monarchs were buried in the Qing-Xiling, a resting place covering 598,000 sq. yd (500,000 sq. m) in Yi county, Hebei. The whole mausoleum complex contains the tombs of four Qing emperors (Yongzheng, Jiaqing, Daoguang and Guangxu), three empress, seven princes and a number of imperial concubines. The tombs here are more scattered than those at Qing-Dongling but are considered architecturally more interesting and are set against a pleasant backdrop of wooded hills.

Admission:
- 8:00~17:30 (Apr. 1~Oct. 31)
- 8:30~17:00 (Nov. 1~Mar.31)
- ¥ 122/Adult
- ¥ 62/Student
- 0312-4710012
  0312-4710016
  0312-4710038

Beijing

Must-try Foods Introduction

At one time, Beijing boasted the largest number of restaurants of reputation, and as a result, an abundance of good food followed. History has seen restaurants and people's tastes change, but many well-established names are as charming as ever, even after hundreds of years of vicissitudes.

Two cultures have had a deep impact on the dining table of the people of Beijing. One of these is that of the Manchu nationality. Many famous barbecue restaurants and Mongolian lamb hot pot restaurants originate from Muslim ones. It was the very primitiveness and lack of regulations that attracted people to barbecued food in the first place. Put up a huge grill, throw a towel over your shoulder to wipe the sweat, put one foot on a stool and use long chopsticks to turn the meat. Add some leeks and garlic to flavor the meat, and then the meat has a bond smoky flavor. This is what barbecue is really about. Today, these procedures are looked after by the waiters and waitresses. All you have to do is to partake. It's convenient, but some of the charm is lost.

The Man culture also endows Beijing with many royal dishes and royal snacks, such as kidney bean rolls, pea flour cakes and *lüdagun* (glutinous rice rolls with sweet bean stuffing). Beijing cheese—soft, cool and creamy—is one delight that is particularly popular in summer.

Lu-style cooking is very influential in Beijing's home kitchens—especially the techniques of flash stir-frying in oil, soup, or water. Also flash stir-frying with salt, sweet sauce, or sweet and sour sauce. Other commonly used techniques are sautéing with rice wine sauce, braising, grilling and blanching. Some typical dishes are: Beijing roast duck, flash stir-fried mutton with leeks, sea cucumber braised with leeks, and sautéed fish slices with rice wine sauce.

The Beijing culinary world is getting ever more sophisticated. According to a survey, the Beijing catering market is now dominated by Sichuan cuisine, followed by Yue cuisine and Shanghai cuisine. Traditional Beijing cuisine is in the fourth place. While people from the rest of the world are bringing new cooking concepts and vitality to Beijing, the hundred-year-old names are still shining, attracting everyone who comes to the city.

Quanjude
quan ju de

全聚德

Founded in 1864, a Lu-style restaurant known for its roast duck snacks. In fact, it is the most famous roast duck restaurant in the country and has become a symbol of Beijing.

Quanjude Premium Roast Duck in Two Dishes/Four Dishes

Ingredients: Duck.
Taste: The signature dish of this hundred-year-old restaurant, it is known for the crispy duck skin and tender meat. The restaurant still follows its traditional methods of duck selection and fruit wood sourcing to assure quality. On the other hand, to cater to the appetite of the modern palate, it has reduced the greasiness of the ducks and come up with more wrapping options, including corn pancakes and green vegetables. For the novice, we recommend the wheat pancakes with leeks, as it is the simplest way of appreciating this dish.
Legend: During the Southern Song dynasty (1127–1279), roast duck was already popular amongst both the common people and government officials. It is documented that

after the Mongolians seized Lin'an, the capital of the Southern Song dynasty, the Mongolian general Boyan relocated hundreds of local craftsmen of different industries to its capital Beijing (or Dadu as it was known at the time). This included roast duck chefs. Roast duck soon became a favorite with the Mongolian royal family. By the Ming dynasty, it had become a must-have in the royal celebration dinners for the Lantern Festival. It was also a favorite of Emperor Qianlong and Empress Dowager Cixi of the Qing dynasty. Hence came the name Beijing Duck. As times change, it is now once again a delicacy that the common people also enjoy.

Hepingmen Branch
🏠 Building 14, Qianmen West Street, Xuanwu District, Beijing
📞 010-63023062 63018833-1151

Qianmen Branch
🏠 No.32 Qianmen Street, Chongwen District, Beijing
📞 010-67011379 65112418

Asian Games Village Branch
🏠 Building 309, Huizhong Bei Li, Chaoyang District, Beijing
📞 010-64801686 64801685

Wangfujing Branch
🏠 No.9 Shuaifuyuan Lane, Wangfujing Street, Dongcheng District, Beijing
📞 010-65253310 65228423

Shichahai Branch
🏠 Shichahai Sports School, No.57 Di'anmen Street, Xicheng District, Beijing
📞 010-66171570 66128557

Tanfu Cuisine Restaurant
tan shi guan fu cai
谭式官府菜

A "feudal official" restaurant that incorporates both Chuan and Yue cuisines, it is ideal for business banquets. Braised shark's fin in yellow wine sauce is one of its standout dishes.

Braised Shark's Fin in Yellow Wine Sauce

Ingredients: Shark's fin, duck, old hen, dried scallop, cured ham.
Taste: One of the masterpieces of the Tanfu cuisine, the dish features tender and translucent shark's fin that tastes savory and smooth. To prepare the dish, a complete shark's fin is carefully selected and blanched in salted water several times to remove the fishy smell. It is then braised on low heat for six to seven hours to fully cook the fin and bring out the flavor. The chef must make sure that enough water is in the casserole dish, because no water or soup should be added during braising. Due to the long braising time, seasonings are added only when the fin is ready.
Legend: The Tanfu cuisine was passed down from the family of Tan Zongjun, a member of the Qing Imperial Academy. An avid gourmet, Mr. Tan relished banquets. His son was even more passionate. His wife and chefs, therefore, spent a lot of time studying various famous dishes, and finally came up with the Tanfu cuisine.

🏯 Wangzuo Center, No.2 South Guandongdian Street, Chaoyang District, Beijing
✆ 010-65617388

Donglaishun
dong lai shun
东来顺

Located in the New Dong'an Market, this well-established mutton restaurant is as traditional as its décor, attracting customers with its large hotpots.

Mongolian Blanched Mutton

Ingredients: Rib, sirloin, silverside, rump and top round of quality sheep bred in the Xilin Guole region of Inner Mongolia.

Taste: The mutton is sliced into uniform, thin pieces on which you can see the grain of the meat. Dip a slice into the dried shrimp and mushroom soup, and it cooks—fragrant and tender, without smell or grease. It is even more aromatic if you have it with the restaurant's home-made sweetened garlic and sesame clay oven pancakes.

Legend: The founder of the restaurant was a vendor named Ding Deshan of Hui Nationality. He started his business serving mutton noodles and sliced buckwheat cakes in Dong'an Market back in 1903. Baked corn cakes and rice porridge were

added later. As his business prospered, he branded his stall "Donglaishun Porridge," indicating that he started in the east of the capital, and hoped that he would prosper in the future. Flash stir-fried mutton, roast mutton, Mongolian blanched mutton and stir-fried dishes were added in 1914, and the name was changed to Donglaishun Mutton Restaurant. With a famous chef and skilled assistants, the restaurant soon gained a strong foothold.

🏠 Floor 5 apm Building, No.138 Wangfujing Street, Dongcheng District, Beijing
📞 010-65280932 65280501

Kao Rou Ji
kao rou ji
烤肉季

This venerable Muslim restaurant is located near Shichahai. In addition to the barbecued mutton, DIY grill sets are available in the private VIP rooms on the top floor for the diners to enjoy themselves.

Barbecued Mutton

Ingredients: Quality black-head round-tail sheep from Xikou, western passes of the Great Wall—only rib, tenderloin and other tender parts of the sheep are selected (20 kg of the total weight).

Taste: The mutton is sliced uniformly and paper-thin. Dip the mutton slices in the sauces, made from soy sauce, vinegar, crushed ginger, rice wine, shrimp sauce, sliced spring onion and coriander, then place on the grill. Turn regularly. Eat it with the sweetened garlic and cucumber strips. It is delightful and aromatic.

🏠 No. 14 Qianhai Dongyan, Shichahai, Xicheng District, Beijing
📞 010-64042554

Man Fu Lou
man fu lou
满福楼

Another well-known Muslim restaurant in Beijing, this one specializes in Mongolian hotpot and is also renowned for its sliced beef hotpot and seafood, not to mention its traditional Chinese décor.

Mongolian Hotpot

Ingredients: Quality top round of sheep from Xilin Guole, Inner Mongolia. Only 2.4 kg mutton out of an 80 kg sheep is used for the hotpot.
Taste: Here the traditional big hotpots are replaced by small pots. The mutton slices are tender and fresh, enhanced by sauces made from 28 flavorings.
Legend: On one of his expeditions, Kublai Khan of the Yuan dynasty missed the delicious "stewed mutton" and ordered his chef to prepare it for him. However, enemy attacks were reported before the dish was ready. The chef sliced the mutton into thin pieces, dipped them in boiling water, and sent them along with some sauces to the hungry Emperor. After defeating his enemies, Kublai Khan named it "Mongolian Hotpot."

No.38 Di'anmennei Street, Xicheng District, Beijing
010-64030992 64043773

Baodufeng
bao du feng
爆肚冯

The best known blanched cow/sheep tripe in Beijing, this restaurant was established more than a hundred years ago during the Guangxu reign of the Qing dynasty. Fresh and tender with thirteen home-made sauces and choices from more than a dozen parts of the innards, it is a popular treat across the country.

Blanched Tripe with Three Different Sauces

Ingredients: Sheep tripe, cow tripe, sesame sauce, soy sauce, vinegar.
Taste: Thinly slice the *duren* (the fleshy part of a cow/sheep stomach) and the *duling* (a horizontal stalk-like structure in the stomach—these are the best grade of tripe. One plate of *duling* comes from six or seven sheep). Then dip in boiling water briefly, and it is ready. The timing must be precise, as different parts of the tripe require different boiling times. If too long, it is overcooked; too short, it is undercooked. Perfectly cooked tripe tastes tender and fresh. Eating it accompanied by home-made sesame sauce, soy sauce, or vinegar with diced coriander, spring onion and spices brings out its flavor.

Legend: This snack was popular among civil officials, the families of the Eight Banners, and especially the opera actors during the Qing dynasty. It could be very simple, or as exquisite as Baodufeng's.

No.6 Guangnei Street, Caishikou, Xuanwu District, Beijing (West of Fenghua Square)
010-83558088

Bianyifang

bian yi fang

便宜坊

This long-established roast duck restaurant enjoys the oldest history amongst all the establishments in Beijing. It is also the only roast duck restaurant that has stuck to its traditional *menlu* roasting method; the duck is roasted in a closed oven—very environmentally friendly by today's standards.

Roast Duck with Vegetable Fragrance

Ingredients: Lake duck.
Taste: Invented by a high-class chef, this dish features rich and juicy duck slices with thick layers of grease. Local Beijing people believe that it is the grease layer that is the key to a genuine roast duck. A crucial step in preparing the dish is to marinate the duck in celery juice to extract the extra grease. The pancakes go with radish sprouts, Chinese toona leaves, mint and other green vegetables instead of leeks. Carrot juice and celery juice are also put in the pancake dough.
Legend: The restaurant started its business in the Ming dynasty, in the 14th year of Emperor Yongle's reign. It was named Bianyifang, this name reflecting its mission to create a convenient (*fangbian*) and pleasing (*yiren*) dining environment with good value food beyond the price for its customers. It was said that the owner had seven courts during the Qing dynasty—five as parlors, one for the owner and his family, and one for the ducks.

🏠 Floor 3 No.5 Chongwai Street, Chongwen District, Beijing
📞 010-67088680

Chang'an Yihao
chang an yi hao

长安一号

One of the new generation of roast duck restaurants, this restaurant is known for its elegant dining environment wherein the patrons can enjoy exquisite dishes while observing the cooks preparing their food in a clean and bright open kitchen.

Traditional Beijing Fruitwood Roast Duck

Ingredients: Lake duck.
Taste: The meat is tender with a special aroma, as the duck is fed with

water that is used to steam dates. Only 35–40 ducks are for sale every day. The ducks are also served cut in a different way: one plate with the skin only, a second one with meat only and a third with the meat attached to the skin. Dip a piece of the skin in white sugar and wrap it around the meat any way you prefer.

Xinjiang Mutton Pancake

Ingredients: Mutton, flour.
Taste: A sophisticated version of this popular Xinjiang snack, there is no

gamey odor and it in fact smells very fragrant.

Desserts

Ingredients: Ice cream.
Taste: The restaurant has a variety of famous desserts. The innovative Wuliangye liquor chocolate ice cream is outstanding.

🏠 Floor 1, Grand Hyatt Beijing, 1 East Chang' an Avenue, Dongcheng District, Beijing
✆ 010-65109608

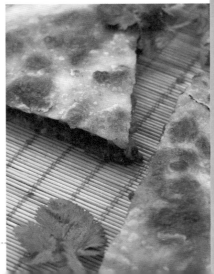

Dadong
da dong
大董

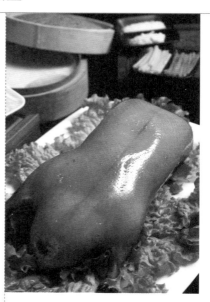

Located in Nanxincang—the royal barn, this restaurant has a 600-year history, which is evident in features such as the heavy vermeil automatic glass door. Adjacent to the door is an open kitchen that is always stocked with several hanging roast ducks.

Dadong Roast Duck

Ingredients: Duck.
Taste: The modern roast duck is less greasy and healthier than its traditional peers. Before you eat, dip the golden crispy skin in white sugar. The crispy skin will melt the sugar on the tip of your tongue, eliminating any greasy feeling. Then wrap the meat, the skin, some spring onion and sweet paste together in a pancake. It is moist and tender. If you prefer a stronger flavor, you can also add some mashed garlic and other sauces.

Tuna Avocado Rolls

Ingredients: Tuna, avocado.
Taste: A fusion dish with ingredients from different countries, it fuses subtle textures and the nutty, cheesy taste of the fruit with the freshness of seafood.

Baked Sea Cucumber with Leeks

Ingredients: Sea cucumber.
Taste: One of the head chef's best, it is also a classic Lu-style dish. The sea cucumbers are soft and smooth, yet chewy. Rich in collagen, this dish is also a healthy food.

Floor 1-2, Nanxincang International Plaza, 22A Dongsishitiao, Dongcheng District, Beijing
010-51690329

Huangting
huang ting
凰庭

This restaurant's design is inspired by the traditional courtyard houses of the families of Beijing nobility. The bricks were taken from hundred-year-old houses that were dismantled in the old districts of Beijing. The tables and chairs are scented rosewood replicas of furniture from the Ming dynasty, and all the other wood pieces are reminiscent of an era gone by. The pine panels and support beams are from a courtyard house in Suzhou. The heavy front door and its iron knockers are all over 200 years old. This restaurant provides a charming retreat to an ancient time.

Haihu Shark's Fin in Crab Meat Stock

Ingredients: Haihu shark's fin, crab meat.
Taste: Boil the fresh crab meat till it is just cooked, and stew the Haihu shark's fin in stock to taste. It is fresh and full-flavored.

Shaomai with Crab Roe, Shrimps and Minced Pork

Ingredients: Crab roe, shrimp, pork.
Taste: *Shaomai* (steamed dumpling with the dough frilled at the top), a masterpiece of traditional Yue-style dim sum—born in a Beijing courtyard house, it combines the fresh fragrance of the shrimp and pork with the dry fragrance of the roe.

Kung Pao Shrimp Ball

Ingredients: Prawn.
Taste: Fresh prawns cooked with sweet garden peas, the dish tastes moderately spicy, fresh and chewy.

B2, The Peninsula Beijing, No.8 Goldfish Lane, Wangfujing Street, Beijing
010-85162888*6707

Jasmine Restaurant and Lounge
mo li
茉莉

Mustard Peas Mixed with Wood Ears

Ingredients: Wood ear, mushroom, pea.

Taste: The colloid-rich wood ears are fresh. With a dash of vinegar, flavored brine and Japanese sake and soy sauce, they are crisp, cool and refreshing, with both sweet and sour flavors. The pungent mustard taste is also refreshingly cool in the hot summer.

In the lobby is the symbol of the restaurant—a Jasmine tree from Africa. It envelops the restaurant in its sweet fragrance from early summer all the way to autumn. Furnished with three-story-high wine racks, a huge classic black crystal lantern and ring-shaped candle sticks, the restaurant truly stands out from its peers.

Martini Braised Lamb

Ingredients: Lamb leg, martini.
Taste: A modern creation, this entree uses the strong flavors of a martini to counteract the gaminess of lamb. Served in a cocktail glass, it looks very appealing. It is very popular with foreigners.

Laksa

Ingredients: Prawn, scallop, chicken, citronella, *Sanba* sauce, coconut starch.
Taste: The rich orange laksa is very appealing to the eye. Originating from Southeast Asia, Laksa is made of citronella and other spices, giving it a mouthwatering pungent taste. It goes well with rice noodles and bean sprouts. The Jasmine Restaurant combines it with a special rice noodle from Yunnan, and different seafood, resulting in a glowing tropical island dish.

East Gongti Road, Chaoyang District, Beijing (opposite Gate No. 10 of the Workers' Stadium)
010-65538606

Duck de Chine
quan ya ji
全鸭季

Featuring traditional Chinese round tables, this restaurant, though not luxurious, is impeccable in its details. From the tablecloth to the table spoons, everything is well-chosen. Near the entrance is a small champagne bar where you can enjoy your roast duck complemented by champagne—the essence of fusion.

Roast Duck

Ingredients: Duck.
Taste: Traditional Beijing roast duck is given a modern twist in this chic restaurant.

Pumpkin in Preserved Sweet Plum Sauce

Ingredients: Pumpkin, preserved sweet plum.
Taste: The sweet and glutinous pumpkin pieces are soaked in the sour, salty and sweet plum sauce. It tastes fresh and delicious.

Scrambled Duck Eggs with Truffles

Ingredients: Truffle, duck egg.
Taste: The eggs are served in a glass, and each diner is served one spoonful. Mixed with olive oil, scrambled duck eggs, truffles and cheese, it tastes rich and creamy.

Club 1949, Courtyard 4, North Gongti Road, Chaoyang District, Beijing
010-65018881

Stop2: Xi'an

Xi'an

Must-go Places Introduction

General Information

Xi'an is the Provincial capital of Shaanxi Province in the central-northwest region of China. As one of the seven ancient capitals of China, it was the capital of 13 dynasties from the time of the 11th century BC rule of the Western Zhou (1046 BC–771 BC) to the triumph of the Tang (AD 618–AD 907). Xi'an is also known for being the eastern terminal of the Silk Road and the location of the terra-cotta army.

Environment

It is located in the hinterland of China, at the lower reaches of the Yellow River. It is surrounded by the Qinling Mountains and Weihe River. The continental climate makes it cold and dry in winter. Except for the winter, any season is relatively suitable for travel. The average temperature is 0°C or above in January and around 25°C in July, with an average annual rainfall between 500~800 mm.

Places of Interest

"The 5,000-year history of China is mirrored in Xi'an." Shaanxi is one of the most important cradles where the Chinese civilization was concentrated. As early as 1 million years ago, the Lantian Man settled down and lived there. In this "natural history museum," there are not only the relics of the ancient Chang'an City, the legendary tomb of Emperor Huangdi, the Qianling Mausoleum, Maoling, the Tomb of Wudi of the Han dynasty (206 BC–AD 220), but also the Forest of Stelae, Huaqing Pool, and the Great Wild Goose Pagoda. The once buried terra-cotta warriors and horses are one of the world's great wonders.

The northern Shaanxi Plateau features the typical Loess Plateau arts and customs, the classic and sonorous Xintianyou folksong, the energetic and brisk waist-drum dancing, delicate paper cutting, and the novelty-rich Chinese peasant painting.

The natural landscape of Shaanxi is equally unmatched. There is the West Sacred Mountain of Huashan, Lishan Mountain in Lintong, Tiantai Mountain in Baoji, Yellow Emperor Tomb, Qiachuan in Heyang, and the torrential Hukou Waterfall of the Yellow River. The river was described by famous poet Li Bai this way—"See how the Yellow River's water pours down from heaven."

www.xian-tourism.com

Xi'an City Wall
xi an cheng qiang
西安城墙

From the 3rd century BC, Xi'an was a vital commercial center because of its position on the eastern stretches of the Silk Road. Its trading importance and its vulnerability—lying in the path of the main Central Asian conduit into the heart of central China—also made it one of the most heavily fortified cities of the north.

From its earliest days, a defensive wall encircled it, and in 1374 when the large program of defensive works was undertaken by the Ming, the city's present wall was built—a massive stone structure, strengthened with fortifications, running about 7 mi. (12 km) around Xi'an, rising 40 ft (12 m) high and spreading 45 to 60 ft (14 to 18 m) thick at its base. They include some 98 watchtowers and nearly 6000 crenels cut into a parapet that runs right around the top of the wall. There are four huge gates, over which the Ming dynasty engineers built small multistory forts with observation points and firing ports, from which teams of archers and other defenders could shower the attacking forces with arrows, gunpowder bombs and blazing oil and naphtha.

Admission:
- South Gate:
  8:00~20:30 (Mar.1~Apr.30)
  8:00~21:30 (May.1~Oct.30)
  8:00~19:00 (Nov.1~Feb.28)
- Moon City:
  8:00~20:30 (May.1~Oct.15)
  8:00~18:00 (Oct.16~Apr.30)
- Wenchang Gate:
  8:00~20:00 (May.1~Oct.15)
  8:00~18:00 (Oct.16~Apr.30)
- Heping Gate (Peace Gate):
  8:00~21:00 (May.1~Oct.15)
  8:00~18:00 (Oct.16~Apr.30)
- East, West, North Gate:
  8:00~20:00 (May.1~Oct.15)
  8:00~18:00 (Oct.16~Apr.30)
- Shangde Gate, Small South Gate:
  8:00~18:00 (All Year Round)
- ￥40
- 029-87282976

Terra-cotta Army
bing ma yong

兵马俑

The vast tomb of Emperor Qin Shihuang, the first Chinese emperor to unify China's warring clans 2000 years ago, might never have been discovered since its highly skilled designers had hidden it extremely well. There is some evidence that long ago grave robbers inadvertently set fires in their search for treasures, but the tomb commissioned by Emperor Qin Shihuang lay quietly 15 to 20 ft (4.5 to 6.5 m) below the Earth's surface, covered by a roof built with layers of fiber mats followed by many feet of soil to conceal it. There is speculation that the tombs workers and supervisors were buried alive at completion to protect its secrets. In 1974 peasants near Xi'an uncovered evidence of the tomb's fabulous terra-cotta army when digging a well. Their well excavation was over an area of the tomb with more than 8000 life-size terra-cotta warriors. The warriors' infinitely varied details of facial features, hair, dress, rank, and the horses for cavalry divisions

meant that no two were alike. The figures had been fired at higher than usual temperatures for terra-cotta and were shaped by using cleverly carved molds to allow for hollow torsos, heads and arms. The legs were solid terra-cotta needed to support each figure's overall weight of up to 600 lb (300 kg). Experts believe this terra-cotta army is only a small part of the buried treasures of Emperor Qin Shihuang's tomb since it lies approximately less than a mi. (1000 m) east of the main tomb. The main entrance to the tomb has still not been located even to this day.

Admission:

🕐 8:30~17:30 (Mar.16~Nov.14)
8:30~17:00 (Nov.15~Mar.15)
¥ 90 (Mar.1~Nov.30)
¥ 65 (Dec.1~Feb.28)
📞 029-81399001
@ www.bmy.com.cn

Qianling Mausoleum
qian ling
乾 陵

Magnificent stone lions guard the entrance to this, the burial place of Emperor Gaozong and Empress Wu of the Tang dynasty. The mausoleum, hewn out of three hills, lies at Liang Mountain in Qian County, Shaanxi. Besides the stone lions, ostriches, winged horses and soldiers that surround the tomb, there are statues of 61 leaders of regional ethnic minorities and foreign diplomats of that time. Emperor Gaozong died in AD 684, and his queen 22 years later.

Admission:
🕐 8:00~20:00
¥ 46 (Mar.16~Nov.14)
¥ 26 (Nov.15~Mar.15)
✆ 029-35510222

Forest of Stelae
bei lin
碑 林

In the Tang dynasty, when Xi'an was called Chang'an, the city was noted for its large collection of stone stele, many of them featuring fine examples of early Chinese calligraphy or carvings of the 13 Classics of Confucian philosophy. In the year AD 904, it was decided that the entire collection should be brought under one roof, so to speak, and a place was reserved within the city wall. But it took another 186 years for work to be completed on Xi'an's Forest of Stelae, a sprawling complex of exhibition halls, covered corridors and a pavilion, which nowadays houses more than 1000 stelaes and tomb tablets.

The exhibition virtually encompasses the history of Chinese writing, presenting the calligraphy of the Qin dynasty (221 BC–206 BC) of the 3rd century BC, through the Tang and Song and into the Ming and final Qing reigns. In 1555 powerful earthquake caused extensive damage to the halls, and the complex was rebuilt at the end of that century. Three new halls were added during the 17th and 18th centuries.

The impressive collection includes all the representative styles of Chinese calligraphy, such as the ancient official script, the highly abstract cursive script and the artistic writings of the great painter-poets, all of which became models for later students of calligraphy. Some of the stelae on display are of great historical value, such as the stela recording the introduction of Christianity into China. Another remarkable stela is a bas-relief called the Four Steeds of Zhao Mausoleum. It is in fact the tombstone of Taizong, the second emperor of the Tang dynasty, and shows the four splendid warhorses that he rode in campaigns against the northern "ethnic minority groups."

Admission:
🕐 8:00~18:45(Summer),
8:00~18:00(Winter)
¥ 45 (Mar.16~Nov.14),
¥ 30 (Nov.15~Mar.15)
✆ 0910-82271080

Yellow Emperor Tomb
huang di ling
黄帝陵

agriculture and the father of the Chinese race itself. His tomb in Qiaoshan in Huangling County, Shaanxi, was built in the Song dynasty to replace an earlier monument set up in the time of the Han. At the foot of a hill close to the tomb there are 14 cedar trees, one of which is said in legend to have been planted by the Yellow Emperor himself. A large plaque in the main hall bears the inscription First Ancestor of Humanity.

Admission:
🕑 8:00~19:00
¥ 91 (Mar.16~Nov.14)
¥ 51 (Nov.15~Mar.15)
☏ 0911-5212742

The Yellow Emperor is credited with being the father of traditional Chinese medicine, the inventor of

Great Wild Goose Pagoda
da yan ta
大雁塔

During their reigns it was customary for successful candidates in the civil service examinations to be entertained at the nearby Apricot Garden and then taken to the Great Wild Goose Pagoda for their signing ceremony. It became a great honor for scholars to "sign at the Great Wild Goose Pagoda," and the poet Bai Juyi (AD 772–AD 846) went one step further than that: "Of those who signed beneath the Great Wild Goose Pagoda, seventeen in all," he wrote, "I was the youngest."

Admission:
🕐 8:00~19:00
¥ 25 (¥20 for the tower)
📞 029-85535014
@ www.xiandayanta.com

This magnificent pagoda south of Xi'an was built by the Buddhist monk Xuanzang (AD 602–AD 664) to store the sutras that he brought from India during the first flowering of the religion in China. The pagoda takes its name from a compelling incident, recorded in Tripitaka's biography, in which a flock of wild geese flew over a monastery in Magadha, a kingdom in Central India. One of them broke its wings and fell from the sky. The monks, believing that it was a Bodhisttva, buried the goose and built the pagoda in its honor.

The pagoda had only five stories when it was first built, and two others were added in the time of the Five dynasties. It bears inscriptions by the Tang emperors Taizong and Gaozong.

Little Wild Goose Pagoda

xiao yan ta

小雁塔

Located in Jianfu monastery, close to the southern gate of Xi'an, the Little Wild Goose Pagoda has a most tumultuous history—it has been struck by no less than 70 earthquakes since it was first built in the year AD 707 and has survived every one of them. According to the city's records, one of the tremors in 1487 was so violent that it left a split 1ft (a third of meter) wide right down the middle of the tower. But 34 years later it was struck—and this time the action of the quake closed the crack. But the pagoda hasn't survived completely unscathed. It was originally 15 stories high, but earthquakes destroyed the two top floors.

In Jianfu Monastery there hangs a large bell that was cast and installed in the Ming dynasty. A beautiful poem pays tribute to its toll:

Frost accompanies the
grayish break of dawn,
On which is painted the still
dallying moon.
My dream is broken by the
sound of the monastery bell,
Which for ten centuries
haunted the mystic air.

Admission:
🕐 8:00~17:00
¥ 50
📞 029-85238029

Drum Tower
gu lou
鼓 楼

While Western medieval towns and forts had night-watch sentries to call the hours of the night, a large drum on the upper floor of this two-story tower in Xi'an boomed out the coming of darkness. The Drum Tower was built in 1380 in the reign of the Ming emperor Taizu and was renovated twice in the following centuries. It is remarkably well preserved and is one of the historic showpieces of a city whose name is synonymous with Chinese history.

Admission:
🕐 9:00~17:00
¥ 27
📞 029-87274580

Huaqing Pool
hua qing chi

华清池

One of the eight most celebrated places of natural beauty in Central China, Huaqing Pool is also the location of a hot springs system that is steeped in history and legend. The first Qin emperor is said to have built a traveling lodge beside the springs, which are found on the slope of Mount Li in the south of Lintong County. According to folklore, on one of his visits, he encountered an immortal disguised as a common peasant woman, who, taking exception to his rather familiar behavior toward her, spat in his face. The emperor's features immediately broke out in a dreadful skin ailment. Apologizing profusely for his indiscretions, the emperor begged her to remove the curse—and the woman revealed herself as an immortal and bathed his face in the spring, curing him as swiftly as he has been afflicted. Thereafter, the hot springs of Mount Li were known as the Immortal Hot Springs.

Another of the springs, called Hibiscus, became the trysting spot of the Tang emperor Xuanzong and his beautiful concubine Yang. The poet Bai Juyi, in his poem *Song of Everlasting Woe*, describes how the "streams of the warm fountain caressed her waxen limbs."

Admission:
🕐 8:00~16:00
¥ 70 (Mar.1~Nov.30), ¥ 40 (Dce.1~Feb.28)
✆ 029-83812003
@ www.hqc.cn

Xi'an

Must-try Foods Introduction

The birthplace of Chinese culinary culture, Xi'an occupies an important position in Chinese culinary history. For more than 1,000 years, in order to indulge the appetites of the rulers, Xi'an produced and attracted a number of well-respected master chefs. They brought with them various cooking techniques, innovative dishes and banquet menus. In addition, business people around the country also brought the best of their hometown dishes to Xi'an. Thanks to the fusion that resulted, Shaanxi cuisine is uniquely positioned to serve as the basis of Xi'an and China's culinary culture.

Xi'an cuisine can be roughly categorized into two types: snacks and formal dishes. The latter includes Shaanxi dishes which are collectively known as the "father of all Chinese dishes" and foreign dishes (both inside and outside China) that are tinged with Shaanxi characteristics.

Shaanxi cuisine is as bold, rustic and simple as its people. It is straightforward, but can also be refined and exquisite. Though not one of the top eight cuisines of China, it is well-known around the country. In terms of taste, Shaanxi cuisine features sour, spicy and savory flavors and aromas. Cooking techniques include steaming, stewing, braising, blanching, quick-frying and stir-frying. It is at the same time both rich and refreshing.

Shaanxi has more varieties in its snacks than any other parts of China. The varieties of the wheaten food alone are overwhelming. It is said that if you are in Xi'an over a period of several months, you never eat the same thing twice.

Xi'an Hotel
xi an fan zhuang
西安饭庄

of the most unique local snacks, it is creamy white and puffy, a silky cloud. Seen from afar, the dumpling looks like a bubble, hence the name Bubbly Lard Dumpling.

Yellow Osmanthus Flavored Persimmon Cake

Ingredients: Huojing persimmon, flour, bean paste, yellow osmanthus.
Taste: Brownish-yellow in color, it is sticky and sweet with the fragrance of osmanthus. It is also a very special local snack.
Legend: It is also known as Huojing persimmon cake. In 1644, Li Zicheng

This is the place to be if you want to have a taste of Shaanxi's local culture and local food. Established in 1929, it is known for its genuine and thoroughly Shaanxi flavors. Its menu offers thousands of choices, including traditional and modern Shaanxi dishes, innovative foreign dishes, as well as local snacks.

Bubbly Lard Dumpling

Ingredients: Flour, lard, bean paste.
Taste: The taste is all its own. One

founded his Dashun regime in Xi'an and went on to attack Beijing. As it was a disastrous year with little harvest, people in Lintong fed the army with persimmon cakes made from persimmons and flour. Today's version is the result of years of refinement of this same cake.

Thousand-layer Shortbread

Ingredients: Flour, Sichuan pepper powder.
Taste: As its name indicates, this type of shortbread is made up of many layers. The dough is stretched and wound many times, then spiraled into shape and put into the oven to bake. When done, it is golden in color, crisp and savory.
Legend: Known as the "Number One Snack in Chang'an (modern-day Xi'an)." During the Tang dynasty, after Monk Xuanzang returned to Chang'an from his long pilgrimage to India with thousands of rolls of Buddhist

scriptures in hand, the emperor of the time, Gaozong, ordered the royal chef to make thousand-layer cakes with vegetable oil for the monk as a gesture of appreciation for his hard work.

Gourd-shaped Chicken

Ingredients: Young chicken, Chinese cinnamon, Sichuan pepper, aniseed.
Taste: Golden color, crispy skin,

tender meat and rich fragrance.
Legend: Known as the "Number One Dish in Chang'an." The name of the dish comes from the gourd shape of the cooked chicken. The dish was created in the Tang dynasty. Wei Zhi, a minister of the Department of Rituals, was very particular about his meals, especially the tenderness of his chicken. His first chef tried deep-frying chicken after boiling, but it was too tough. The second chef tried boiling, then steaming and finally deep-frying it. It was tender and crispy, but the chicken and the bones were separated. The third chef learned his lesson from his predecessors and bundled the chicken when cooking. It was tender, crispy, and fragrant with a delicious, lingering aftertaste—and, of course, shaped like a gourd.

Sliced Kidney Cooked at Moderate Heat

Ingredients: Sliced kidney, vermicelli.
Taste: This dish requires precise slicing, accurate flavoring and perfect water temperature control. Timing is also of the essence when blanching the kidney slices.
Legend: This is an improvement on the dish Kidney in Wine and Vinegar found recorded in a book of cookery from the Tang dynasty. It is now a representative dish of the art of cooking at moderate heat.

Banquet: Shaanxi Snack Banquet

Main Dishes: Green onion and ground meat cake, steamed meat dumpling, pan-fried chives dumpling, *shaomai* with three fillings, steamed vegetarian dumpling, steamed bun roll, thousand-layer shortbread, bubbly lard cake, tower-shaped shortbread, yellow osmanthus flavored persimmon cake, mustard leaf spring roll, date paste, winter sweet steamed dumpling with squid filling, sea cucumber *shaomai*, juicy *baozi* (steamed stuffed bun) with

scallop filling, chrysanthemum shortbread, *Yiwosi* cake, shrimp dumpling with paper-thin skin, Empress Dowager cake, *Xiangna* of Yulin, the walnut bun of the Wang Family of Ningqiang, Fufeng cake with venison, Fengxiang tofu pudding, decorated buns, butterfly-shaped sea cucumber, gourd-shaped chicken, orchid-shaped egg rolls filled with faat choy, quick-boiled mushroom with walnut, creamy fish soup, sliced kidney cooked at moderate heat, etc.

Reasons of Recommendation:
Also known as the "Kaleidoscope of Shaanxi." this is a special collection of approximately 70 Shaanxi snacks from hundreds of snacks all over the province, some signature dishes of the restaurant and other well-known dishes.

Building on traditional cooking techniques, the banquet integrates the best of various cooking schools, exquisite in both technique (including steaming, deep-drying, pan-frying, roasting, boiling, etc.) and appearance. The ingredients used vary with the seasons, and the dishes have a variety of different tastes: salty, sweet, sour, spicy, savory, fragrant and crisp. Each dish, be it hot or cold, with meat or vegetarian, is of a different taste and style.

Headquarters
No. 298 East Street, Beilin District, Xi'an
029-87680883

Fenggao Road Branch
No.30 East Fenggao Road, Lianhu District, Xi'an
029-84295768

Heping Road Branch
No.138 Heping Road, Xincheng District, Xi'an
029-87680899

Lao Sun Jia Restaurant
lao sun jia fan zhuang
老孙家饭庄

Founded in 1898, this restaurant is representative of Muslim cuisine in Shaanxi and the northwest of China as a whole. Known as the "Premiere Bowl of the World," it specializes in shredded pancake in mutton or beef broth, Muslim dishes, and snacks of the local ethnic minorities. It is even said that the two main things you must do in Xi'an is to visit the terra-cotta warriors and have the shredded pancake in mutton broth in Lao Sun Jia restaurant.

Shredded Pancake in Mutton or Beef Broth

Ingredients: Processed beef or mutton, pancake, beef or mutton broth.

Taste: The essence of the food culture along the ancient Silk Road, this dish is the best-known Muslim snack in Shaanxi. It features rich broth that is slow-cooked, savory mutton or beef, a chewy pancake, intense color and a strong fragrance.

Legend: It evolves from the mutton and beef broths of the 11th century BC. At that time, broth was listed as one of the ritual gifts presented to princes and lords.

Crisp Roast Lamb Leg

Ingredients: Foreleg of lamb, seasoning.
Taste: Based on a dish made for lamb banquets as found recorded in a book of cookery from the Qing dynasty, it is golden in color with crisp skin and savory and tender meat.

Sesame Tenderloin

Ingredients: Raw mutton or beef, egg, white sesame.
Taste: Golden in color, soft and tender, fragrant and savory.

Ethnic Restaurant of West China Branch
No.78 Dongguanzheng Street, Beilin District, Xi'an
029-82494851
Xiwu Road Branch
No.26 Xiwu Road, Xincheng District, Xi'an
029-87421858 87433131
East Street Branch
No.364 East Street, Beilin District, Xi'an
029-87214438
Great Goose Pagoda Branch
North Square of Great Goose Pagoda, Xi'an

Qinyu Hamburger

qin yu rou jia mo

秦豫肉夹馍

pork.

Taste: The salted pork is made by stewing quality pork in brine seasoned with over 20 flavorings including cloves, Chinese cinnamon, aniseed and dittany bark. The final product is deep red, soft and tender, rich but not greasy. The pancakes are made by hand, and are crisp and fragrant.

This is a popular Shaanxi hamburger restaurant recommended by local Xi'an people.

Qinyu Hamburger

Ingredients: Baked pancake, salted

No.19 Dongmutoushi, Beilin District, Xi'an

Tianxia Diyi Mian
(Best Noodles in the World)
tian xia di yi mian
天下第一面

This restaurant specializes in 18 types of noodles, 28 varieties of snacks, 88 cold dishes and 108 hot dishes originating from Qishan, Shaanxi.

First Noodle

Ingredients: Noodle, abalone and shark's fin soup, sour and spicy minced pork soup.

Taste. The restaurant is named after this noodle dish. The dough is pressed from both the top and bottom with thick wood bars to make the noodles "as thin as paper, as soft as tendon." The sour and spicy minced pork soup is an improvement over traditional minced pork soup and tastes sour,

spicy and rich. One bowl of noodles goes with two types of soup.

Legend: The name was given by an American visitor over ten years ago who wrote "Best Noodles in the World" after he tried the noodle in the restaurant. Later, Liu Wenxi, a famous calligrapher and painter, wrote the Chinese version of the name after eating the noodles here.

Pork Bones Braised in Soy Sauce

Ingredients: Fresh pork backbone.
Taste: Simple backbones may seem ordinary but these are very tasty. To truly enjoy them, you must gnaw on the bones.

Xifu Liquor Platter (Pork Braised with Vegetables)

Ingredients: Pork butt, wood ear, daylily, hawkweed, turnip, potato.
Taste: Farm-produced red vinegar from Baoji is added as the pork is stir-fried, reducing the greasiness of the pork fat and tenderizing the meat.

Jixiangcun Branch
No.195 Hanguang Road, Yanta District, Xi'an
029-85398299

Wenchangmen Branch
No.19 Dongmutoushi, Beilin District, Xi'an
(20 m east of Luomashi Nankou)
029-87286088

East Xiaozhai Road Branch
No.32 East Xiaozhai Road, Yanta District, Xi'an

Wei's Liangpi
wei jia liang pi
魏家凉皮

Wei's Liangpi was founded by Wei family who came from the Hanzhong area. They combined the family's traditional way of making *liangpi* with the Qinzhen style and created the Wei's *liangpi*, which has been popular ever since.

Liangpi

Ingredients: *Liangpi* (Rice sheet), flour sheet, chili oil.

Taste: Refreshing and slippery, the *liangpi* is fragrant with chili oil. The thin, white rice sheets mixed with bright red chili oil look inviting. Two kinds of sheets are available—rice

and flour. The rice sheets are soft and slippery, while the flour sheets are chewy.

Legend: Qinzhen rice sheets have a history that can be traced back to the Qin dynasty (221 BC–206 BC). Back then, they were an article of tribute for the emperor. Hanzhong *liangpi* was invented in the Qin and Han dynasties when the farmers made thin savory pancakes by diluting the dough with water and adding spicy sauces.

Shaanxi Hamburger

Ingredients: Baked pancake, salted pork.

Taste: Shaanxi hamburger is the best choice to go with *liangpi* and porridge. The pancake dough is hand-kneaded and baked. The pork is slow-cooked. It is a real treat.

Floor 1, Xuelinyayuan, South Daxue Road, Beilin District, Xi'an (near Bianxi Street)

029-62273752

Jiasan Juicy Baozi
jia san guan tang bao zi
贾三灌汤包子

Known for its varieties of dishes and exquisite cooking, this is a classic Muslim restaurant.

Jiasan Juicy *Baozi*

Ingredients: Corn flour, fruit and vegetable, Qinchuan beef, and prairie mutton.

Taste: With corn, fruit and vegetable dough, Qinchuan beef or prairie mutton filling, the *baozi* is juicy with rich soup broth. Wrapped in a special way, it has a paper-thin skin, juicy and tender meat and rich juice. It is shaped like a pomegranate or *yuanbao* (an ancient Chinese gold or silver ingot), as translucent as jade and when it is picked up with chopsticks, it looks like an ancient Chinese sachet. All these shapes are Chinese symbols of luck and fortune.

Huimin Street Branch
No.93 North Yuanmen, Huimin Street, Lianhu District, Xi'an
029- 87257507
Great Goose Pagoda Branch
C-05 North Square of Great Goose Pagoda, Yanta District, Xi'an

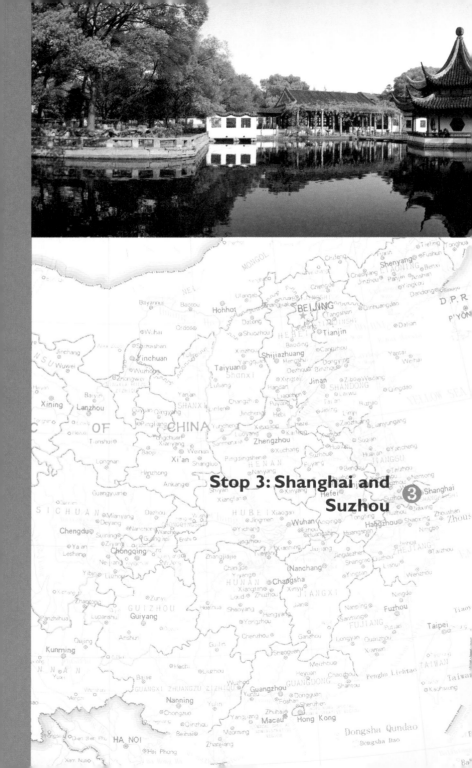

Stop 3: Shanghai and Suzhou

Suzhou
Must-go Places Introduction

General Information

Suzhou is one of the oldest cities on the lower reaches of the Yangtze River and on the shores of Taihu Lake in Jiangsu Province.

A large area of the city is covered by water, including a vast number of ponds and streams. Taihu Lake, four-fifths of which is in the territory of Suzhou, is one of the four largest fresh lakes in China. The city is cut by the Beijing-Hangzhou Grand Canal from north to south.

Since the Song dynasty, Suzhou has been an important center for China's silk industry and continues to hold that prominent position today.

Environment

About 80%~90% of Jiangsu Province's territory are plains, the lowest and flattest land in China. Suzhou is influenced by the northern subtropical humid monsoon climate. The average temperature is 2~8°C in January and 26~32°C in July, with an average annual rainfall between 800~1,200 mm.

Places of Interest

Suzhou is an ancient city with a 2500 years' history. It's "a very great and noble city ... It has 1600 stone bridges under which a galley may pass." (Marco Polo) Strolling on the streets, you can feel the unique charm left by its long legacy.

Suzhou's classic gardens reveal the heart and soul of the city. The classic gardens—full of poetic and artistic expression by traditional Chinese freehand brushwork paintings—are made through the elaborate arrangement of rocks, water, vegetation, and layout of the buildings. These gardens were named UNESCO World Heritage Sites in 1997 and 2000. At present, more than 60 gardens are kept intact here.

The exquisite water townships in Suzhou are rated by tourists alongside classical gardens. Zhouzhuang, Mudu, Tongli towns should not be missed by any visitor. In any water township of Suzhou, a number of Ming and Qing dynasties preserved buildings can be found. The natural scenery and human landscape enhance each other's beauty, providing a peaceful oasis for visitors.

Taihu Lake
tai hu
太湖

The Taihu Lake is the third biggest freshwater lake in China and is famous for its rocks—strange and somewhat bizarre natural formations that have been used all over China to decorate parks and gardens. It is also where Fan Li, the mastermind who help the Prince of Yue to inflict vengeance on the Prince of Wu in 476 BC, is said to have celebrated his victory by taking the most coveted beauty of that time, Xi Shi, for a boat ride. The lake covers 926 sq. mi. (2400 sq. km) and spreads into the provinces of Jiangsu and Zhejiang. It is mainly fed by two streams, the Tiao and Jing and empties through many others into the Yangtze River. There are 48 small islands in its waters, and peaks of 72 hills parade around it.

Han Shan Monastery
han shan si
寒山寺

Han Shan Monastery in Fengqiao, Suzhou, dates back to AD 502–AD 519, but was destroyed by fire several times over the centuries, and its present structure goes back only to the beginning of this century. Its name is said to have come from the monk Han Shan, who came to the area with a colleague, Shi De. Gilded statues of both men are housed in its great hall. The Tang dynasty poet Zhang Ji immortalized the monastery in lines that spoke of "the sound of the midnight bell (coming) to my lonely boat." The monastery bell disappeared a long time ago, and a replacement installed in the Ming dynasty has also gone—it is now in a collection in Japan. A new one hangs in Han Shan monastery, which was made in Japan and donated to the monastery.

Admission:
- 7:00~17:30 (Mar.20~Oct.19)
  7:00~17:00 (Oct.20~Mar.19)
- ¥ 20
- 0512-65348048

Tiger Hill Pagoda
hu qiu
虎丘

Built in the middle of the 10th century on Tiger Hill in Suzhou, the eight-sided seven-tiered tapering pagoda is constructed of bricks but in the style of traditional wooden structures. In 700 years, from the 12th to 19th centuries, it suffered seven major fires that badly damaged the top and all the eaves. What remains now is the basic brick structure, which requires constant maintenance. First named the Yunyan Pagoda, it is probably the oldest of its design south of the Yangtze River. The pagoda stands 164 ft (50 m) high, and every floor is accessible by a wooden staircase.

On every story of the pagoda, there are murals of peonies. Other features, such as the cantilevered brackets and coffered ceilings, are also painted over with rather special designs.

Admission:
🕐 7:30~17:00
¥ 60 (Apr.16~Oct.30), ¥40 (Oct.31~Apr.15)
📞 0512-65323488
@ www.tigerhill.com

Humble Administrator's Garden

zhuo zheng yuan

拙政园

Another famous Suzhou residence, the Humble Administrator's Garden, was built in 1513 by a retired civil servant, Wang Xianchen, on the site of the former Dahong Monastery. He took its name from a poem on leisurely living by Pan Yue of the Jin dynasty, a line from which goes: "To water the garden and grow vegetables is a form of government by the simple soul." Renovated in the Qing reign, this is now the largest and most splendid residential garden in Suzhou. Since its first occupant, it has had some illustrious owner-residents, including the grandfather of the novelist Cao Xueqing (author of *A Dream of Red Mansions*) and Li Xiucheng, a leader of the Taiping Revolution against Qing rule.

Admission:
🕐 7:30~17:30
¥ 70 (Apr.16~Oct.30), ¥ 50 (Oct.31~Apr.15)
✆ 0512-67510286
@ www.szzzy.cn

Tips:
A portable e-guide can be rented at the entrance. After you leave the Humble Administrator's Garden, a 100-m walk to the west will take you to the Royal Prince House of the Taiping Heavenly Kingdom, the Suzhou Museum, and the Suzhou Gardens Museum. Walk another 100 m south along the Garden Road to get to the Lion Forest Garden and the Suzhou Folk Culture Museum.

Lion Forest Garden
shi zi lin
狮子林

Lying adjacent to Humble Administrator's Garden and covering an area of 1.1 hectare, the garden was first constructed in the 2nd year of Zhizheng in the Yuan dynasty (1342). Its name came from the Buddhist doctrine. Both Emperor Kangxi and Emperor Qianlong of the Qing dynasty paid several visits to the garden and made a replica of it respectively in the Yuanmingyuan Park of Beijing and the Imperial Summer Mountain Resort of Chengde. The impressive and labyrinthine artificial limestone rockworks in the garden boast deep caverns and zigzagging paths. The whole garden is compactly laid out with corridors leading to all directions and small paths opening upon an enchanting view. It has also tall and graceful ancient trees.

Admission:
🕐 7:30~17:00
¥ 30 (Apr.16~Oct.30), ¥20 (Oct.31~Apr.15)
📞 0512-67773263
　　0512-67272428
@ www.szszl.com

Tips:
The Lion Forest Garden is near the Suzhou Folk Culture Museum and the Museum of Banknotes and Coins. You can tour these two places together with the Garden. A 100-m walk to the north will take you to the Humble Administrator's Garden.

Couple's Garden Retreat

ou yuan

藕园

The Couple's Garden Retreat has three sides facing water, with the eastern side facing the river. With the canal running through both front and back, this garden retains the classical characteristics of Suzhou Jiangnan water towns. The exterior of the Couple's Garden Retreat is the best-preserved in Suzhou. Shen Bingcheng, the founder of the Couple's Garden Retreat, resigned under the pretext of illness and moved to Suzhou with his young wife Yan, where he rebuilt the Couple's Garden Retreat on the site of a garden from the early Qing dynasty which had gone to waste.

Unlike other residential gardens that separate residential and scenic parts, the residential part of the Couple's Garden Retreat is in the center of the garden with two separate gardens situated on the east and west sides, to signify husband and wife. It is the only example of a dozen buildings being interconnected by winding walkways.

Admission:
🕐 7:00~17:30
¥ 20 (Apr.16~Oct.30), ¥15 (Oct.31~Apr.15)
📞 0512-67272717

Tips:
The Couple's Garden Retreat, the East Garden and the Zoo are offered as a combination tour.

Master-of-nets Garden
wang shi yuan
网师园

Suzhou has for centuries been known as one of central China's most beautiful cities and the place where wealthy mandarins, merchants and landowners built fine retirement residences, many of them connected to the network of lakes and canals that have given the city the reputation of being the Venice of the East. Master-of-nets Garden, a particularly well-designed and opulent garden home, was built by Shi Zhengzhi of the Song dynasty and was named Ten Thousand Volumes Hall at first. In 1736 it was bought by Song Zongyuan, who changed its name to Fisherman's Recluse and chose Wang Shi (Master of Nets) as the name of its garden. With its cottages, pavilions, studios and ponds, it embodied all that the wealthy retired required of life—visual pleasure and harmony.

Admission:

🕐 7:30~17:30 (Mar.1~Nov.15)
🕐 7:30~17:00 (Nov.16~Feb.29)
¥ 30 (Apr.16~Oct.30); ¥ 20 (Oct.31~Apr.15)
　Night Garden:
　19:30~22:00 (Mar.10~Nov.20) ¥ 80
📞 0512-65293190
@ www.szwsy.com

Tips:

An Evening Garden Tour is one unusual feature of this garden. Classical entertainment such as Kunqu Opera and traditional storytelling are offered. You can view traditional stringed and woodwind Jiangnan (south of the Yangtze River) instruments such as the *zheng* (an ancient Chinese plucked musical instrument) and bamboo flutes on display in the various halls around the garden.

West Garden
xi yuan
西园

This palatial residence complex and garden in Liuyuan Street, Suzhou, has a colorful and complicated history. First built between 1522 and 1566 by a retired Ming dynasty mandarin, it was then converted to a monastery by his son; then, in the 19th century, it was demolished and rebuilt in its present form. It still includes the monastery, and a main hall that houses the images of 500 arhats and a statue of the monk Ji Gong, whose face, viewed from the right, has an amused, happy expression, but from the left is sad. Viewed from the front, it appears to be happy and sad all at once. The pond that links the various buildings is well stocked with colorful carp and is home to a tortoise said to be over 300 years old.

Admission:
🕐 7:30~16:00
¥ 25
📞 0512-65349545

Lingering Garden
liu yuan
留园

Located outside of the Changmen Gate and covering an area of 2.3 hectare, it is one of the four most famous gardens in China. A retired bureaucrat first constructed the garden during the reign of Wanli (1573–1620) in the Ming dynasty and then it was renovated during the late period in the Qing dynasty. The garden is celebrated for its exquisite and artistic division of architectural space with halls, corridors, whitewashed walls and tunnel portals. The seemingly divided areas, combined with stones, water and vegetation, form a variety of interlocking courts, which exhibits an artistic feature of gardens south of the lower Yangtze.

The Lingering Garden is divided into four scenic areas: the Middle Area, the East Area, the West Area and the North Area, interconnected by a 700-m long zigzag corridor. Both sides of the long corridor are adorned with over 300 sq. m of stone carvings featuring calligraphy from many dynasties, and are known as the Orthodox Calligraphy Models of the Lingering Garden.

Admission:
- 🕐 7:30~17:30 (Mar.20~Oct.19)
- 🕐 7:30~17:00 (Oct.20~Mar.19)
- ¥ 40 (Apr.16~Oct.30), ¥30 (Oct.31~Apr.15)
- ℂ Tel: 0512-65579466
- @ www.gardenly.com

Garden of Cultivation
yi pu
艺圃

"A garden earns more fame with a better owner." The Garden of Cultivation is an unusual gem because it remained unchanged despite its various owners. Therefore, even though it is small, the garden is part of the World Heritage list. Three well-known scholars possessed the garden: Yuan Zugeng (1519–1590) of the Ming dynasty, who stepped down from his position in the government at the age of 40 to become a widely respected scholar; Wen Zhenmeng (1574–1638), who served as the prime minister in the late Ming dynasty, enjoyed a high reputation as the great-grandson of Wen Zhengming, a celebrated master painter in China's history; and Jiang Cai, a respected scholar and minister of Foreign Affairs during the late Ming dynasty, who protested against corruption by exiling himself.

The Fish-feeding Pavilion of this garden is the only example of Ming dynasty architecture to have survived through the years. Ancient colored

drawings and floral designs remain intact on the roof beams of the pavilion. Take some time to appreciate these precious rarities.

Admission:
- 🕐 7:30~17:00 (Mar.21~Nov.15)
- 🕐 7:30~16:30 (Nov.16~Mar.20)
- ¥ 10
- ✆ 0512-67271614

Stop 3: Shanghai and Suzhou

Shanghai

Must-go Places Introduction

General Information

Shanghai, the largest city in China, is located at the mouth of the Yangtze River. Its phenomenal economic growth in the last 15 years is the talk of Asia and the entire world. The start of the boom began in 1990, and it seems like the skyline of the city changes every month. In the 1920s and 1930s, Shanghai was known as the Paris of the East, but upheaval and war left the city in disarray. Now Shanghai has regained its luster, luring people from all over the world to visit and invest. Shanghai is a place "where yesterday meets tomorrow."

Environment

The vast majority of Shanghai's land area is flat, apart from a few hills in the southwest corner. Shanghai has a humid subtropical climate and experiences four distinct seasons. The most delightful seasons are spring, although the weather conditions can change quickly, and autumn, which is generally sunny and dry. The average temperature is $1\sim8°C$ in January and $23\sim32°C$ in July.

Places of Interest

The Bund, located along the bank of the Huangpu River, contains a rich collection of early 20th century architecture.

Pudong, literally meaning east of the River lies across from the Bund, exemplifies the most dramatic changes in modern Shanghai. Ten years ago Pudong was mostly rice and vegetable fields, but it has transformed into Shanghai's newest business and residential area, spreading out from Lujiazui, the finance and trade center of the metropolis. The historic classical architecture of the bund and modern skyline of Lujiazui creates an exciting contrast for Shanghai's many visitors.

In Puxi, literally meaning west of the River, the city's historic row home neighborhoods called *shikumen* have been refurbished to preserve the essence of Shanghai living during the 1930s. Xintiandi (New Heaven and Earth) located in downtown is the typical successful example. It is a chic area with trendy shops, restaurants and cafes for local fashion lovers and visitors alike.

http://lyw.sh.gov.cn/en/

Yu Garden
yu yuan
豫园

Yu Garden, a classical garden in downtown Shanghai, dates back over 400 years. Each pavilion, hall, stone and stream in the garden expresses the quintessential South China landscape design from the Ming and Qing dynasties. From over forty spots —divided by dragon walls, wood corridors and beautiful flowers— visitors can take in the garden's many scenes. Strolling in the garden evokes the phrase, "one step, one beauty; every step, every beauty."

Yu Garden occupies an area of 20,000 sq. m (about 5 ac.). Although the small size does not represent the attractions of the garden, its pavilions, halls, rockeries, ponds and cloisters all have distinctive characteristics. There are six main areas in the garden: Sansui Hall, Wanhua Chamber, Dianchun Hall, Huijing Hall, Yuhua Hall and the Inner Garden. Each area features several scenic spots within its borders.

The surrounding bazaar is packed with traditional and modern shops, restaurants and a temple.

Admission:
🕐 8:30~17:30
¥ 40 (Apr.1~Jun.30, Sept.1~Nov.30)
¥ 30 (The rest months)
📞 021-63282465

Nanjing Road
nan jing lu
南京路

Nanjing Road of Shanghai, known as "China's premier shopping street," stretches around 5.5-mi. from Jing'an Temple in the west to the Bund in the east. The East Nanjing Road pedestrian mall was completed at the 50th anniversary of the People's Republic of China. Huge shopping centers, specialty stores and shops with Chinese specialities line both sides of this street. Shanghai No. 1 Department Store, Hualian Department Store, Shanghai Fashion Co. LTD., and Shanghai No. 1 Foodstuff Store are four major companies that reflect the past and present of Nanjing Road, making it a shopping experience combines traditional and modern styles. West Nanjing Road is known for its luxurious shopping centers, which offer countless famous brands, superior quality, and new fashions. Walking along Nanjing Road, one will find one of the city's most vibrant parts. Flashing neon signs, the fashionable stores flanking the street, the hustling and bustling crowd, the lovely sightseeing trains, the uniquely-designed city sculptures, all reflect the modern urban side of Shanghai.

Oriental Pearl TV Tower
dong fang ming zhu
东方明珠

The Oriental Pearl Radio and Television Tower is 468 m tall. It has 11 big and small spheres. Besides its height, the tower's impressive architectural design also makes the Oriental Pearl TV Tower an eye-catching feature to the Lujiazui skyline. The entire building is supported by three gigantic columns,which are 9 m in diameter each and start underground. The entire structure rests on rich green grassland and gives the appearance of pearls shining on a jade plate. Together with the Nanpu Bridge and Yangpu Bridge on the Huangpu River, it looks like two dragons playing with a ball.

The various spheres and columns actually house places of interest, commerce, and recreation. Shanghai Urban Historical Development Gallery is on the first floor. The large lower sphere has a futuristic space city and a fabulous sightseeing hall. The pearl at the very top of the tower contains shops, restaurants, including a rotating restaurant, and a sightseeing floor. At nighttime, the tower becomes a brilliant three-dimensional sight, which amazes every visitor.

Admission:
- 🕐 8:00~21:30
- ¥ 100 (to the 263-m-high Sightseeing Hall)
- ¥ 135 (to the 90-m-high Big Siphere and the 263-m-high Sightseeing Hall)
- ¥ 150 (to the Three Main Spheres)
- ✆ 021-58791888

Jinmao Tower

jin mao da sha

金茂大厦

Standing in the Lujiazui financial and business district the Jinmao Tower faces the Bund across from the Huangpu River. With a total height of 420.5 m and 88 floors above ground, the Jinmao Tower—generally regarded as a landmark building of Shanghai—combines elements of Chinese culture with the latest in architectural design.

The observation deck on the 88th floor at 340.1 m covers an area of 1,520 sq. m. The glass wall offers panoramic views all over the city and a magnificent vista of the Yangtze River's estuary.

This is one of the tallest atriums in the world—a barrel-vaulted atrium, starting from the 56th floor to the 87th. The two express elevators escalate at 9.1 m per second, sending tourists to the top of the building in only 45 seconds.

Admission:
- 🕐 8:30~22:00
- ¥ 88
- 📞 021-50475101

The Bund and the Huangpu River
wai tan, huang pu jiang
外滩　黄浦江

The Bund shows off Shanghai's outstanding buildings that line the Huangpu River of different architectural styles, including Gothic, Baroque, Romanesque, Classicism and the Renaissance. It stretches one mile along the bank of the Huangpu River. Traditionally, the Bund begins at Yan'an Road in the south and ends at Waibaidu Bridge in the north, while crossing over the Suzhou Creek. This row of 52 structures—known as a museum of "buildings in multinational styles of architecture" for combining the Oriental and Occidental—has been regarded as an important landmark in Shanghai for over a century. At night, floodlights illuminate the attention to detail in each building's design. Nowadays, the Bund is one of the most trendy places in Shanghai, featuring world-class luxury brands. It's a favorite haunt for fashion lovers and the affluent.

The Huangpu River, the largest river and the most important shipping artery of Shanghai, twists and turns like an undulating muddy dragon from the mouth of the Yangtze River to the East China Sea. The yellow and ice-free Huangpu River is 114 km (71 mi.) long, 400 m (0.25 mi.) wide and has an average depth of 9 m (30 ft). The river divides the city into two parts: Puxi (west) and Pudong (east). Whether it is during the day or at night, the views along the river are beautiful. The great modern skyscrapers of Pudong and the classical buildings in different architectural styles in Puxi are records of development during various historical periods. The Huangpu River is a witness for it all.

Shanghai Museum
shang hai bo wu guan
上海博物馆

Located on the southern grounds of People's Square, the Shanghai Museum is one of the four major museums in China, garnering the same fame as the Palace Museum, Nanjing Museum, and Xi'an Museum. The museum building with a round top and square base is shaped like an ancient bronze tripod cooking vessel called a *ding*, symbolizing the ancient Chinese perception of the world as a "round sky, square earth."

It has an exhibition area of 12,000 sq. m on four floors. The first floor features the Ancient Chinese Bronze and the Ancient Chinese Sculpture galleries; the second floor has the Ancient Chinese Ceramics gallery; the third floor contains the Chinese Calligraphy, Chinese Painting, and Chinese Seal galleries, and the fourth floor features the Ancient Chinese Jade, Chinese Coin, Chinese Ming and Qing Furniture, Chinese Minority Nationalities' Art galleries. Currently, the museum has a collection of 120 thousand pieces of precious and rare works of art, including bronze, ceramics, calligraphy, furniture, jades, ancient coins, paintings, seals, sculptures, minority art and foreign art, which narrate China's 5,000-year civilization.

Admission:
- 9:00~17:00 All Year Round (Entry stops at 16:00)
- ¥ Ticket Free, Admission Fee for Special Exhibitions: ¥20
- 021-96968686
- @ www.shanghaimuseum.net

Xintiandi
xin tian di
新天地

Located in downtown Shanghai, Xintiandi is a fashionable entertainment pedestrian zone that reflects the city's historical and cultural legacies. This urban complex brings together modern buildings with *shikumen* homes, the main residential homes for Shanghai residents in the early 1900s. It covers an area of 30,000 sq. m. The old *shikumen* underwent restoration to integrate with the new buildings around. The results are preserved *shikumen* exteriors with interiors that embody a different world of international galleries, bars, cafes, boutiques, and theme restaurants, which combine history, culture, tourism, business, entertainment, and residences. The contrast and integration of the past and the present, and of the East and West give Xintiandi an endless charm. It has been an ideal place for foreign and domestic tourists to have a general view of the history, culture, and modern lifestyle of Shanghai, and the best place for people of refined taste to meet and enjoy city life.

Ancient Town of Zhujiajiao
zhu jia jiao
朱家角

Zhujiajiao is an ancient town located in a suburb of Shanghai at the bank of Dianshan Lake. The town, with a history of over 1,000 years, is the most well preserved ancient town in Shanghai and has been known as the "Venice of Shanghai" In 1991, it was designated by the State Council of China as a "Well-Known Chinese Cultural Town."

It has a simple, but attractive appearance typical of towns in southern China. People who live amidst the hustle and bustle of modern city life can find antiquity, lersure and tranquility among the old stone bridges crossing the bubbling streams, small dark-awning boats, weeping willows swaying along the riverbanks, and Ming and Qing styled residences with inviting couryards.

Walking along the zigzagged narrow streets and lanes lined with shops and stores, tourists feel like they're strolling through a simple, but lively wash painting. Exquisite in structure and beautiful in shape, Fangsheng Bridge is the first of the ten attractions in Zhujiajiao. Constructed in the reign of Emperor Wanli of the Ming dynasty, it is the largest joint five-arch stone bridge in Shanghai.

Admission:
- 🕐 8:00~16:00
- ¥ 80 (for 9 Scenic Spots, including Touring Boat)
- ¥ 60 (for 8 Scenic Spots)
- ¥ 30 (for 4 Scenic Spots)
- ✆ 021-59240077

Shanghai Grand Theater
shang hai da ju yuan
上海大剧院

The Shanghai Grand Theater is located on the west side of People's Square, next to the Shanghai Municipal Building in the East.

Designed by well-known French architect Jean Marie Charpentier, it combines the Eastern and Western elements in concise and graceful geometrical forms, such as the crown-like white arc-shaped roof bending upwards. It looks like a modern-day crystal palace in the light at night. With its forward style and beautiful outlook, the theater has become a representative building in Shanghai.

On the top of the building, there are outdoor theaters and a mid-air garden that is in the shape of a treasure bowl. The Grand Theater is made up of three parts with a total floor space of 70,000 sq. m. The lyric theater for ballet, musical and symphony performances has 1,800 seats divided into the auditorium, the 2nd and the 3rd-floors, and six balconies. The drama theater has 750 seats and the studio theater has 300 seats. Moreover, the Shanghai Grand Theater also has 12 rehearsal halls, gymnasiums, scene-setting rooms, make-up rooms, banquet halls, cultural exhibition halls, and underground garages.

Shanghai

Must-try Foods Introduction

By the early twentieth century, local Shanghai cuisine (*Benbang Cai*) had formed through the convergence of flavors from sixteen places, including Suzhou, Wuxi, Nanjing and Anhui.

Local Shanghai cuisine combines features unique to areas south of the Yangtze River. First, only fresh local fish, shrimp and vegetables are used. Second, different dishes are prepared for each season: alfalfa, wolfberry leaves, bamboo, Pacific Saury and long-nose catfish are used in spring; steamed Hilsa herring and sautéed shelled shrimp for summer; sautéed crab meat, pork balls with crab sauce, turtle brewed in rock sugar, double boiled bamboo shoots with salted pork, red braised intestine, and sea cucumbers with shrimp roe in autumn. Third, the usual cooking techniques used are: stewing, steaming, simmering, braising and sautéing. However, nowadays stewing, dry-frying, sautéing with starch sauce (*hua chao*), and steaming are the most popular. Among them dry-frying and sautéing with starch sauce (*hua chao*)

are particularly suitable for fish or shrimp dishes. Fourth, the flavors are diverse, both heavy and light, and all with a typically Shanghainese dash of sweetness and light flavor.

And now, with the increasing cultural exchanges between Shanghai and foreign countries, the Shanghai diet is fusing with traditional cuisines from other areas. On the Bund, and in Shanghai's Xintiandi area, there are many fine restaurants that have more fusion fare on offer than local Shanghainese food. Immigrants from other parts of China to Shanghai (called the new Shanghainese) have also enriched the Shanghai diet with their hometown flavors.

Typical Shanghai snacks have a long history, starting out in the Southern Song dynasty and developing into Shanghai specialties during the Qing dynasty. The snacks are seasonal, featuring different flavors and an array of choices. Careful selection of ingredients and preparation with attention to detail is also a characteristic. The most famous snack of them all is the Nanxiang Steamed Pork Bun(Nanxiang *xiaolong*).

Lao Zheng Xin Restaurant
lao zheng xing
老正兴

It is one of the oldest restaurants serving local Shanghai food. The décor of the restaurant has an air of antiquity, and the food offered here is done in the most traditional Shanghai style.

Marinated Bran Dough with Peanuts and Black Wood Ear

Ingredients: Bran dough, peanut, black wood ear, daylily.
Taste: A classic cold dish in local Shanghai cooking, it is light with no soy sauce flavor, and tastes both sweet and sour. It makes a very good appetizer.

Chili Sauce with Eight Delicacies

Ingredients: Chicken breast, pork tenderloin, tripe, chicken gizzard, shrimp, winter bamboo shoot, peanut, dried tofu slice.
Taste: This is a home-style side dish for most ordinary Shanghai families. The shrimp used in this dish must be fresh and toothsome.
Reasons of Recommendation: Born from the time when food was scarce, it is very popular as its strong taste goes well with bland rice.

Alfalfa with Braised Pork Intestine

Ingredients: Alfalfa, pork intestine.
Taste: This almost looks like a French dish—stir-fried alfalfa interspersed with sections of bright colored pork intestine. The taste is rich but well balanced.
Reasons of Recommendation: This is a simplified version of a Lu-style cuisine—Braised Intestines in Brown Sauce.

🏠 No.556 Fuzhou Road, Huangpu District, Shanghai
📞 021-63222624

Lü Bo Lang Restaurant
lü bo lang
绿波廊

This is an internationally renowned Shanghai-style restaurant, and state leaders are often entertained here. It is said that it was founded during Emperor Jiajing's reign in the Ming dynasty. In the 13th year of the Republic (1924), it was transformed into a tea house. In 1979, it was renovated and made into a restaurant specializing in Shanghai-style cooking. Now it has many branches, but this one in Yu Garden is the most traditional and authentic of them all.

Steamed Sea Cucumbers with Shrimp Roe

Ingredients: Sea cucumber, shrimp.
Taste: The plump, dark but shiny sea cucumbers are thoroughly cooked but not mushy. The juice is dark red and thick.
Legend: It is said that about one hundred years ago, Shanghai people preferred river food to seafood and sea dry food. In the 1920s, the chef of this restaurant, after many attempts, finally created this dish and gave sea cucumbers a place in local Shanghai cuisine. The dish has been popular ever since.

No.115 Yuyuan Road,
Huangpu District, Shanghai
021-63280602 63557509

Dried Salted Yellow Croaker

Ingredients: Yellow croaker.

Taste: Salty, dry and fragrant, this appetizer is known for its strong taste.

Reasons of Recommendation: Fresh yellow croakers were salted and dried. The best Dried Salted Yellow Croaker is pure white in color, round in shape, and fresh in taste; it is neither too salty nor too plain. It is rich in protein but not fatty. People in Dinghai, Zhejiang Province like to cook it with roast pork when entertaining guests.

Bamboo Shoot and Shiitake Mushroom Steamed Bun

Ingredients: Fresh bamboo shoot, shiitake mushroom, green vegetables.

Taste: A home-style dim sum item, the steamed bun is small in size so you won't get too full even if you eat many of them. They are packed with filling and wonderfully fresh.

Crab Meat Steamed Bun

Ingredients: Flour, pork, crab meat.

Taste: These are small, translucent and juicy. They taste best when served with shredded ginger and vinegar.

Legend: This bun was created in 1871 during Emperor Tongzhi's reign in the Qing dynasty. Credit for them goes to Huang Mingxian, born in Nanxiang town. He started out with the humble steamed bun and slowly made over the recipe. He made thin wrappers with refined flour and added lean pork stuffing; instead of MSG, he used chicken soup and pork skin jelly for flavoring. Ground sesame was also added to make it more fragrant. Crab meat, shrimp or spring bamboo shoots were sometimes added, depending on the season. Then one day, he opened his Nanxiang Steamed Pork Bun shop in downtown Shanghai, which has enjoyed a great reputation ever since.

Yangtze Hotel
yang zi fan dian
扬子饭店

This hotel opened in 1934. Built in an Art Deco style, it has become an archetype of the protected architecture of Shanghai. The restaurant consistently cooks the most traditional Shanghai food, and thus is very popular among local customers.

Crystal Sautéed Shelled River Shrimps

Ingredients: Shelled river shrimp.
Taste: The shrimps have a nice chewy texture. They are pure white, plump and tender.
Reasons of Recommendation: Once known as sautéed shelled shrimp, this is a common freshwater food dish in Shanghai and Jiangsu. It became quite popular during the Qing dynasty in South China. With wild shrimp cooked in a traditional style as the main ingredient, this dish has over 20 years of history, and thus has a very nostalgic taste.

Scallops and Shrimps with Cucumber

Ingredients: Cucumber, ox tripe, scallop, grass shrimp.
Taste: An artistic starter, this dish integrates fresh and elegant Japanese ingredients.

Sautéed Lobsters with Fried Shrimps

Ingredients: Lobster, shrimp.
Taste: This dish creatively combines Western lobster with Chinese shrimp. In a single dish, one can enjoy both Chinese and Western styles of cooking.

🏠 Floor 2, No.740 Hankou Road (near Yunnan Road), Huangpu District, Shanghai
📞 021-63517880*1777

Jade Garden Restaurant
su zhe hui
苏浙汇

This is one of the busiest mid-to-upper range chain restaurants in Shanghai. It used to be an old-fashioned restaurant offering traditional local food. Now it boasts some unique qualities: an elegant dining environment and exquisite Shanghai dishes.

Smoked Duck

Ingredients: Duck.
Taste: Prepared mainly in the Sichuan-style, it also applies some creative methods in its Shanghai-style cooking. The resulting taste is different from the run of the mill duck dishes. The duck has a strong tea fragrance.
Legend: Huang Jinlin, a chef in the imperial kitchen of Cixi, the Queen Dowager of the Qing dynasty, was the first man to use camphor leaves and tea leaves to smoke duck. The smoked duck has crispy skin and tender flesh, is dark red in color and has the unique flavors of camphor and tea. It tastes best when the duck is served in lotus leaves seasoned with sweet and sour duck sauce.

Steamed Hilsa Herring

Ingredients: Hilsa herring.
Taste: A dish near extinction, it is known for the glistening silvery scales of the fish and its fatty, fresh and tender meat.
Legend: This dish is one of the favorites of the literati. Originally, restaurants tended to choose Hilsa herring from Fuchun River as the main ingredient and steam them with ham, bamboo shoots and shiitake mushrooms. It would be best if hilsa herring is got during the Dragon Boat Festival (May 5th on the lunar calendar). Because of the thick fat layer beneath the scales is rich in minerals, the fish doesn't have to be scaled. However, now Hilsa herring in Fuchun River are now facing extinction, so restaurants more often use herring from Burma or the United States.

Sautéed Shelled River Shrimp

Ingredients: Shrimp.
Taste: The shrimp are white, chewy and fresh.
Reasons of Recommendation: Evolving from the Longjing tea flavored shrimp of Hangzhou and the Bi Luo Chun tea flavored shrimp of Suzhou, this dish combines the essence of both. The shrimp are tender, and at the same time retain their original taste and flavor.

Crispy Green-tea Pastry

Ingredients: Longjing tea, flour.
Taste: Made of fresh Longjing tea and refined flour, the pastry is stuffed with lotus seed paste mixed with green tea powder, giving off the scent of spring. It is crumbly, fresh and tasty.

🏠 No.127 South Maoming Road, Luwan District, Shanghai
✆ 021-54037028

New Jesse Restaurant
xin ji shi jiu lou
新吉士酒楼

The first restaurant in Xintiandi, it is in a traditional *shikumen* house that was built in 1925. The building is the best-maintained of all the old buildings in this district. The jet-black wooden door, the red lanterns hanging over the entrance, the lights and the shadows, the steady stream of people and the old photos of Shanghai that hang on the second floor—all are reflections of the prosperous old Shanghai.

Red-cooked Pork

Ingredients: Pork.
Taste: Cooked in typical Shanghai-style, it looks oily and heavy, but tastes fragrant, rich and tender.
Legend: In memory of his father who liked both red dates and braised pork, Zengzi, one of Confucius' most famous disciples, invented this Red-cooked Pork by cooking red dates with pork. Later, as the once precious sugar became more easily affordable, and cooking skills improved, people began to replace the dates with sugar. The color of the pork is still as red as the dates, but it tastes softer and richer. It has always been one of the most popular home-style dishes in China.

Stir-fried Vegetables

Ingredients: Baby bok choy, cabbage, wood ear, mushroom, bamboo shoot, carrot.
Taste: Colorful, delicious and rich in nutrition, these vegetables are a feast for both the eyes and the mouth.

🏠 Building 9, No.2 Lane 181, Taicang Road, Xintiandi, Luwan District, Shanghai
✆ 021-63364746

Zhi Zhen Yi Pin Restaurant

zhi zhen yi pin

致真一品

This is an old restaurant serving high quality Shanghai-style food. Its décor combines aspects of both Chinese and Western culture. Secluded and quiet, it is particularly popular with foreign patrons.

Fried Grass Shrimps in Traditional Chinese Gold Ingot Shape

Ingredients: Grass shrimp.
Taste: After shelling the shrimps, you bite into the juicy meat. The longer you chew, the better they taste.
Reasons of Recommendation: This restaurant's version is an improvement over the Shanghai-style stir-fried shrimp. It uses less soy sauce, and the color is lighter and more pleasant. Each shrimp seems to be

bending over into the auspicious shape of a traditional Chinese gold ingot.

Red-cooked Pork of Jiangnan (Regions South of the Yangtze River) Flavor

Ingredients: Pork.
Taste: The pork is from a special kind of pigs found only in Jinhua of Zhejiang Province. It is known for its meaty texture and superior taste.

Braised Bamboo Shoots

Ingredients: Spring bamboo shoot.
Taste: This is the best dish to have in the springtime when the bamboo shoots are fresh and crunchy.

🏠 Building 7, No.1726 Middle Huaihai Road, Xuhui District, Shanghai
☎ 021-64332882

Yuan Yuan Restaurant
yuan yuan
圆苑

All the dishes here are carefully prepared. Their signature red-cooked pork is the best-known of its kind in Shanghai.

Red-cooked Pork

Ingredients: Pork.
Taste: The most popular red-cooked pork in Shanghai, it is heavy and rich in a typical Shanghainese way.

Goose Liver with Sake

Ingredients: Japanese sake, goose liver.
Taste: The goose liver is delicate in company with the clear and cool sake.
Reasons of Recommendation: It is a fashionable trend in China to pair Japanese sake with French goose liver.

Red-cooked Long-nose Catfish

Ingredients: Long-nose catfish.
Taste: It tastes tender and fresh, rich but not greasy. The skin of the fish is particularly chewy.
Legend: Originating from Hubei, the main ingredient of the dish is the long-nose catfish that is found in the section of Yangtze River that starts from Shishou to Jinkou Town. The fish is golden in color, tender and smooth in taste, fragrant and savory. The celebrated writer and poet Su Dongpo wrote a poem dedicated to this nutritious and delicious dish: "There are no bones in the pink Shishou Town, as the white porcupine fish is deliciously free of poison."

🏠 KWah Square, No.108 North Xiangyang Road, Xuhui District, Shanghai
☎ 021-51083377

A Shan Restaurant
a shan fan dian

阿山饭店

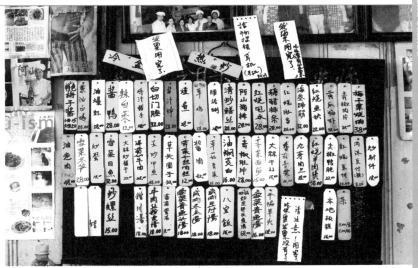

This most grass-root local restaurant in Shanghai is a family-owned business and run by three generations together. It has no branchies, and offers typically rich and heavy home dishes. Though it doesn't look like anything special, it is always full of patrons, both rich and poor.

Boiled Bamboo Shoots with Fresh and Salted Pork

Ingredients: Bamboo shoot, fresh pork, salted pork, dried knotted tofu.
Taste: The tofu knot is fresh and savory in the creamy and thick soup; the spring bamboo shoots are crunchy and refreshing. It is a springtime seasonal dish.

Reasons of Recommendation:
It is in fact a stew of fresh pork and salted pork, mixing the pungent odor of the preserved meat with the taste of fresh meat. The bamboo shoots add to the freshness. In the drizzly southern Yangtze delta, the rich and savory hot soup will warm you up in a delicious way.

Chinese Plum Sauce

Ingredients: Green Chinese plum.
Taste: It is very appetizing and refreshing to eat in the hot summer.
Reasons of Recommendation: It is based on Chef A Shan's secret recipe. When A Shan was young, there were several plum trees in his yard, and in every June his mother would use the plums to make plum sauce for the family to cool them down. Later on, through much trial and error, A Shan finally mastered his trick: The best plum sauce is made by stir-frying and then preserving boiled plums together with white sugar.

Eight Delicacies Rice

Ingredients: Glutinous rice, red date.
Taste: With this extremely simplified Eight Delicacies Rice, you can appreciate the most authentic home-cooking of old Shanghai. The degree of sweetness and the quantity of lard are carefully balanced.

🏠 No.2378 Hongqiao Road, Changning
District, Shanghai
☎ 021-62686583

Legend: After King Wu of the Zhou dynasty (1066 BC–221 BC) defeated his archenemy King Zhou of Shang (1600 BC–1046 BC), he ordered his chef to make this dish as a token of appreciation to the eight cabinet ministers who had contributed the most to his success. The ingredients of the dish vary from region to region. In the south of the Yangtze River, this mild and sweet version is very popular.

Fu 1088 Restaurant

fu 1088

福 1088

This restaurant is in an old-fashioned residential compound comprised of two Spanish three-story garden houses that lead into each other. The arched gate and windows and spiraling pillar ornaments have a Spanish Islamic flavor.

Smoked Fish in Shanghai Style

Ingredients: Herring.
Taste: This is a sweet cold dish served hot. The skin is crisp while the meat is tender.
Reasons of Recommendation: A Suzhou-style dish, its key lies in the brine. It is also a common homey dish in Shanghai families and is a

must-have on the table for New Year's Day and other festivals.

Yellow Croaker and Preserved Vegetables Stewed with Noodles

Ingredients: Preserved vegetables, yellow croaker, noodle.
Taste: The noodle soup is creamy and rich, and the fish tastes smooth and tender. Occasionally, precious wild yellow croakers are used in this dish.

No.375 Zhenning Road, Jing'an District, Shanghai
021-52397878

Dried Salted Eggplant

Ingredients: Eggplant, garlic.
Taste: A non-spicy version of its Sichuan counterpart, it features an attractive presentation and tasty.

Villa du Lac
hu ting
湖庭

It is located in a secluded part of Xintiandi facing Taiping Lake. It serves haute Huaiyang-style food in a simplistic and modern Chinese-accented setting.

Cold Platter

Ingredients: Lettuce, radish, seasoned eel, chicken.
Taste: A combination of Lettuce with Sesame Oil, Sweet-and-sour Radish Rolls, Tea Flavored Red-cooked Eel, and Liquor-marinated Chicken. All the dishes go well with wine and are served in courses, following the "dining pace" of Western dinners. The faint fragrance of the tea compliments the chewy and soft eel. The Maotai liquor in the brine enhances the firm texture of the chicken.

Braised Mandarin Fish with Shredded Dried Tofu

Ingredients: Shredded dried tofu, mandarin fish.

Taste: The art of the cutting is fully presented in this dish. The rich shark bone soup and the fresh mandarin fish set off the unique taste of the shredded dried tofu.

Reasons of Recommendation: It was inspired by the famous dish Braised Shredded Chicken with Ham and Dried Tofu, but the main ingredients have been changed up to give it a stronger Western flavor.

Sautéed Beef Filet with Black Pepper

Ingredients: Beef filet, tofu skin.

Reasons of Recommendation: A fusion of Huaiyang-style food and Western ingredients, it tastes as rich as most Chinese dishes, but has a simpler cooking process. Under the beef filets is a layer of fried shredded tofu skin which tastes particularly savory after marinating in the juices from the meat.

No.373 South Huangpi Road, Luwan District, Shanghai
021-53832998

Whampoa Club
huang pu hui
黄浦会

This restaurant features exquisite presentation of its dishes and fuses new ingredients from all over the world with local Shanghai cuisine. Some of the dishes seem almost outlandish with their foreign ingredients like goose liver and truffle, but in essence they are still very Chinese.

Tomato in Truffle Salt

Ingredients: Tomato, black truffle.
Taste: The unique scent of truffles sets off the fresh and sweet tomatoes.
Reasons of Recommendation: Chef Jereme Leung discovered truffle salt made of truffle and pure sea salt when in Tetsuya Wakuda's restaurant in Sydney. He believes that truffle salt should not be cooked, and that only raw dishes are able to fully realize the flavor.

Duo of Chinese Noodles Flavored with Cuttlefish Roe and Shrimp Roe

Ingredients: Cattlefish roe.
Taste: Cattlefish roe is very special ingredient. Before putting it into the oven to roast, the cook must get rid of its strong fishy odor. When ready, it is taken out of the oven and left to cool, then cut into slices. No seasonings are

added. It goes very well with shrimp roe in the braised noodles. In their creative version of noodles mixed with green onion, the restaurant presents two types of noodles in this one dish—a savory bland noodle and a numbing Sichuan pepper noodle.

Cold Noodles with Numbing Spicy Ice-cream, Fruits and Vegetables in Season

Ingredients: Ramen noodle, ice-cream.

Taste: A dish for summer, it features local noodles of superior quality with Western toppings.

Reasons of Recommendation:
The basic recipe and cooking method is completely Chinese, similar to the noodles with deep-fried sauce, into which small red Sichuan peppers are added. The key revolutionary point here is to replace the traditional sauce with the spicy ice-cream.

🏠 Floor 5, No.3 the Bund, No.1 East Zhongshan Road, Huangpu District, Shanghai (near Guangdong Road)
📞 021-63213737

Tian Di Yi Jia Restaurant
ti di yi jia

天地一家

This restaurant is located on the iconic landmark of Shanghai—the Bund. One of the few premium Chinese restaurants in Shanghai, it is decorated in Art Deco style. Most of the furniture and ornaments in this restaurant are valuable antiques, creating an elegant and tranquil ambience for the customer.

Tea-flavored Smoked Duck

Ingredients: Taihu Lake duck.
Taste: The body of the duck is plump, golden and fragrant. The meat is tender—fatty but not greasy. The skin can be peeled off and melt on your tongue. It tastes best served hot with thin pancakes, leek and sweet bean sauce. It remains crisp, even when it is cold.

Reasons of Recommendation: Only Taihu Lake ducks are chosen as their meat is delicate and low in fat, while the bones are crisp when cooked. Before being smoked, the cleaned duck must be marinated for 12 hours in more than ten seasonings such as tea, nutmeg and so on, and then steamed for two hours. After that the duck is hung over a pot that is used to roast tea and smoked for ten minutes. The final step is to deep-fry the duck. Tea-smoking is the key to this dish, and it gives the duck the flavor unique to the south of the Yangtze River.

Premium Seafood Platter

Ingredients: Prawn from Bohai, sea cucumber from Northeast China, sea crab from the South China Sea, abalone from Australia, deep sea snail, octopus.
Taste: All ingredients are of the highest quality. Served on crushed ice, the dish is served with home-

made Thai sauce. It tastes sour, spicy and a little sweet. Mustard also complements the dish. It is especially good in summer.

Orange Flavored White Gourd and Duck Soup with Rice

Ingredients: Old Duck leg, white gourd.
Taste: A complete set—it includes rice and a platter of four dishes. White gourd is the vegetable for summer. Dried orange peel goes very well with the old duck, as it negates the strong odor of the meat.
Reasons of Recommendation: The fragrant dried orange peel is an ingredient used in traditional Chinese medicine, and is believed to warm the stomach and cool the summer heat. Thus, this dish also has a medicinal effect.

Shanghai-style Ice-cream

Ingredients: Ice-cream.
Taste: An original Shanghai-style

creation, it has a very nostalgic taste.
Reasons of Recommendation: These four flavors of ice cream are all childhood favorites of the generation born in the 1970s and 1980s. The raw ingredients are genuine White Rabbit cream candy, Aquarius carbonated water, Guan Sheng Yuan Lacovo and hawthorn discs. The chef reduces the sugar and fat amounts to make it healthier.

Floor 3, No.6 the Bund, No.1 East Zhongshan Road, Huangpu District, Shanghai
021-63297333

Ye Shanghai Restaurant
ye shang hai
夜上海

Wide arrays of exquisite new Shanghai-style dishes and snacks are offered here. The decor is done up in replica of *shikumen* houses of old Shanghai, but the food is served in the Western way, a typical example of fusion. Its strength, though, still lies in traditional Shanghai-style cooking.

Blanched White Shrimp

Ingredients: White shrimp from Taihu Lake.

Taste: This simple dish retains the original taste and flavor of the shrimp perfectly. Boil water, add green onion and ginger, blanch the shrimp, and it is ready to serve. It tastes even better with a cup of Taidiao rice wine added.

Reasons of Recommendation: This type of shrimp is only about 2–3 cm long, and as small and translucent as a grain of rice. When cooked, it turns light pink. They taste best in late spring and are also known as "the shrimp of Qingming Festival (falls on April 4th, 5th or 6th)."

Pancake Stuffed with Pine Nuts and Mashed Chicken

Ingredients: Pine nut, chicken.

Taste: This snack is this restaurant's original creation. The crunchy pine nuts taste especially savory.

Chicken in Taidiao Rice Wine

Ingredients: Chicken, Taidiao rice wine.

Taste: The strong aroma of the wine combines with the delicate chicken to create an excellent cold dish.

Legend: Once upon a time, there were three brothers in a small village of Zhejiang. The wives of the two elder brothers were both born into rich families and had more than enough dowries, but they were very lazy. The third brother married a poor girl who, though without any dowry, was an able woman, clever and deft.

In order to decide who should run the household, the three sisters-in-law were required to cook chicken without cooking oil or any other ingredients. It turned out that the chicken prepared by the wife of the third brother was the best; the chicken tender and scented with the fragrance of wine. Her secret was Taidiao rice wine. Thus she undisputedly won the right to run the large household.

Unit1,Building 6, Lane 181, Taicang Road, Luwan District, Shanghai
021-63112323

Stop 4: Hangzhou ④

Hangzhou

Must-go Places Introduction

General Information

Hangzhou, one of the seven ancient capitals and a scenic tourism and historic cultural city in China, was once praised as "the most splendid and luxurious city in the world" by Marco Polo, the Italian traveler in the 13th century. Now it's the provincial capital of Zhejiang Province in southeast China.

Environment

Hangzhou is located in the southern part of the Yangtze River Delta, at the western end of Hangzhou Bay, in the lower reaches of the Qiantang River, and at the southern terminus of the Beijing-Hangzhou Grand Canal. Under the subtropical and monsoon conditions, Hangzhou has four distinct seasons with a mild and humid climate and plenty of sunshine and rainfall. The average temperature is 16.2°C round year, 28.6°C in the summer and 3.8°C in the winter. The average annual rainfall is 1,435 mm and the average relative humidity is 76%.

Places of Interest

As a key national tourist destination, and historic cultural city named by the State Council of China, Hangzhou is renowned as a "Paradise on Earth," "Cultural State," "Home to Silk," "Home of Tea" and "Land of Fish and Rice." Some museums reflecting this diverse culture can be found in Hangzhou.

West Lake is undoubtedly the most renowned feature of Hangzhou. There are numerous historical sites and stunning vistas around West Lake. The "Ten West Lake Prospects" have been especially selected to give a visitor outstanding views of the lake, mountains and monuments.

www.gotohz.com

West Lake
xi hu
西湖

Hangzhou and its West Lake have been immortalized by countless poets and artists. The west lake was called Golden Cow Lake before the Song dynasty because a golden cow was said to materialize on its waters whenever a sage or holy man passed by. Later, the poet Su Shi (Dongpo) compared the lake with the famous beauty Xi Shi, writing that like the courtesan: "It is attractive with make-up or without." The lake site used to be a shallow bay connected to the Hangzhou Bay but was gradually sealed off by alluvial deposit, and dredging and landscaping did the rest.

This oval-shaped lake has an area of about 2.3 sq. mi. (6 sq. km) and a circumference of 9.3 mi. (15 km). The average depth of the lake is about 5 ft (1.5 m), with the deepest part being only 9 ft (2.8 m) and the shallowest spot less than 3.3 ft (1 m).

The city of Hangzhou stands on its eastern shore. On the gentle slopes of the hills surrounding the three sides of the lake are large gardens displaying a variety of flora: peach blossom in spring, lily in summer, osmanthus in autumn and plum blossom in winter. The hills are dotted with pavilions, pagodas, grottoes, mansions and streams.

The lake also adds its beauty and mystique to the Ten Beautiful Sites of Hangzhou—Autumn Moon over the Smooth Lake, Spring Dawn on the Su Causeway, Snow over the Broken Bridge, Dusk at the Thunder Peak Pagoda, Evening Bell from Nanping, Waving Lotuses on a Garden Pond, Golden Carp in Huagang, Listening to the Nightingales under Willows on Lakeside, Three Pools Mirroring the Moon and Double Peaks Piercing the Clouds.

Three Pools Mirroring the Moon

san tan ying yue

三潭映月

Three Pools Mirroring the Moon is the largest and finest artificial isle in the West Lake. It is also called the Lesser Yingzhou Isle after a legendary islet in the depths of the Eastern China Sea. The islet covers 7 hectare including the water surface and the area called "a lake within an island and an island within a lake." Three small gourd-shaped pagodas were built afterwards in the south lake of the islet, which is the origin of the name "three pools." A general named Peng Yulin, after retiring from his official post, built for himself a garden villa on the island at the beginning of the Qing dynasty. Zigzag bridges and pavilions were later additions. Three Pools Mirroring the Moon today is the result of a large scale refurbishing project around the end of the Qing dynasty.

The three stone miniature

pagodas standing in the lake off the isle are presumably the best place for moon viewing. On the night of the Mid-autumn Festival, the isle and its three miniature pagodas are a prime attraction for moon spectators. Lights are put inside the windows of the pagoda. The water near the pagoda reflects the shiny lights and the moon. The moon in the sky, water, and hearts of onlookers further accentuates the beauty of this scenic spot.

Admission:
🕐 8:00~17:00
¥ 20
📞 0571-87065684

Bamboo-lined Path at Yunqi
yun qi zhu jing
云栖竹径

This attraction is located southwest of West Lake on the North Bank of the Qiantang River and in the Wuyun Hill Yunqi Village. "Yunqi" means clouds lingering. The Bamboo-lined Path at Yunqi is well-known for its quietness and coolness. Among the trees around the path, one of the Chinese sweet gum tree is over a 1000 years old. Hundreds of thousands of bamboo surround the famous stone-paved footpath leading into the Yunqi valley. Walking along, the Mind Purifying Pond, which means "a pure mind," appears on the path. The cool and clear water, refreshing sounds of nature, and picturesque environment make it a relaxing place for people from the city.

Three ages-old pavilions were constructed to complete the bamboo-lined path: "Mind Purifying Pavilion," "Dragon Back Pavilion" and "Meeting-rain Pavilion." It's a wonderful experience to enjoy the rain while listening to the sound of raindrops beating on the leaves sitting in the pavilion.

In each season, different scenes delight visitors. In spring, shoots grow among the forest; in summer, the cool breeze carries the fragrance of the trees; in autumn, the forest over the surrounding hills turns color; and in winter, the whole valley is cloaked in white.

Admission:
🕐 7:00~18:00
¥ 8
📞 0571-87090437

Spring Dawn on the Su Causeway
su di chun xiao

苏堤春晓

The three km-long Su Causeway became a tourist attraction as early as 1090. It is named after the famous personality who constructed it— Northern Song dynasty poet Su Dongpo, who organized a large scale dredging of the lake and then created causeway with the silt from the dredging during his term as the city's governor. Today's causeway is the result of many refurbishing projects over the centuries.

The causeway consists of six single-span stone arch bridge that offer different views: Yingbo (reflecting the waves), Suolan (locking the waves), Wangshan (looking at distant hills), Yadi (causeway ballast), Dongpu (eastern ford), and Kuahong (spanning rainbow). The embankments along the way are lined with graceful willows and various flowers. Visitors can stand on the causeway and view the lake far and near through the willow branches. In the evening, the causeway is illuminated by lights, making it a romantic spot for promenading couples. In spring, the scenery of Su Causeway is the most enchanting, giving it the specific name "Spring Dawn on the Su Causeway."

Admission:
Ticket free
℃ 0571-87025793

Longjing Tea Fields
long jing wen cha
龙井问茶

Longjing (Dragon Well) Tea is one of the most renowned Chinese green teas. Its name comes from where the best quality tea of this kind is cultivated. The village is right outside Hangzhou. The tea's history and the village are full of legend with the royal family of the Qing dynasty.

The best time for visiting Longjing Tea Fields is during the harvest period, usually from the first week of March until after early May. Farm hands pick the fresh tea leaves throughout the fields. This spring harvest is the best quality to purchase because tea crops later on in the year have had their leaves damaged by rain.

Admission:
🕐 8:00~16:00
¥ 10
📞 0571-87961002

Liuhe Pagoda
liu he ta

六和塔

The Liuhe Pagoda, also known as Six Harmonies Pagoda, stands on the Qiantang River in Hangzhou and was first erected in AD 970 in the belief that it would help placate mischievous spirits and control local flooding. The present brick pagoda was built in 1533, and its wooden eaves were renovated in 1899. The octagonal pagoda is nearly 200 ft (60 m) high, with 104 iron wind bells playing from the corners of its eaves.

Admission:
🕐 6:00~18:30
¥ 20 (¥10 for the Pagoda)
✆ 0517-86591401

General Yue's Temple and Tomb

yue miao

岳庙

Two rows of red-lacquered pillars lead to the main hall of the Temple of General Yue, each engraved with scenes of his most famous Song dynasty battles against Jin invaders. Another engraving displays the characters *xin zhao tian ri* (Heart as Clear as Sun in Sky), based on the general's last words before execution. The seated statue of the great warrior was only recently cast and installed. Over it hangs a plaque inscribed with four Chinese characters *huan wo he shan* (Restore to Us Our Land and Rivers), and the ceiling is painted with more than 370 white cranes, symbolizing loftiness and staunch loyalty.

Admission:
🕐 7:30~17:00
¥ 25
📞 0571-87960089

Peak Flown from Afar
fei lai feng
飞来峰

There are as many as 300 stone carvings that adorn the walls and cave of Peak Flown from Afar near the Lingyin Monastery. The most well-known sculpture is that of Maitreya in the form of the Laughing Buddha. Its name comes from the monastery's founder, the Indian monk Huili, who is said to have commented on a visit there: "This looks a hill of the Immortal Vulture Mountain of Tianzhu. I wonder when it flew and settled here." The sculptures shown here were begun in the Five dynasties (AD 907–AD 960) and added to in the reigns of the Song and Yuan.

Admission:
🕐 6:00~18:30
¥ 35
📞 0571-87969691

Lingyin Monastery
ling yin si
灵隐寺

This famous monastery stands to the northwest of the West Lake in Hangzhou. Its site was selected in 326 (Eastern Jin dynasty) by the Indian abbot Huili, who decided it was a fitting "hermitage for the Immortals." During the Five dynasties following the collapse of Han rule, the devoutly Buddhist Zian Liu, the prince of Yue, greatly expanded the monastery to include nine mansions, 18 pavilions and 3000 monks and novices. When the Qing emperor Kangxi visited the huge complex on his trip to southern China, he gave it the name Cloud Forest Zen Monastery (Yunlin *chansi*). The monastery still features its ornate Great Hall, a 110-ft (33.6-m) high structure that houses a 30-ft (9.1-m) tall gilded statue of Sakyamuni Buddha sitting on a lotus pedestal, based on a well-known sculpture of the Tang dynasty. A lengthy couplet describing famous scenic spots in Hangzhou is inscribed on two tall pillars in front of the statue. The hall is also decked with other images and paintings representing Buddhist mythology, and two ancient stone plaques with inscriptions from the scriptures.

Admission:
🕐 6:00~18:30
¥ 30
📞 0571-88906668

Hangzhou

Must-try Foods Introduction

A famous historical and cultural city, Hangzhou boasts a delicate, well-balanced and open-minded food culture.

Before the Southern Song dynasty established the city as its capital, Hangzhou cuisine had two schools: the "lake school" and the "city school." The former was known for its preference for shrimp, fish, and waterfowl as ingredients. Its usual preparation methods included stir-frying stewing, and quick-frying. Its focus was on light, crisp, fresh and tender tastes and the original flavor of the ingredients. Its signature dishes include West Lake Fish in Sweet and Sour Sauce, Stewed Turtle, Fish with Spring Bamboo Shoots, Stir-fried Swamp Eel Slices, Broad Beans with Diced Ham, Water Shield Leaves Soup and Drunken Shrimp. The "city school" was distinguished by its preference for meat. Techniques included steaming, braising, blanching and simmering. The typical tastes were light, fresh, tender and savory. Its best dishes included Fish Head with Tofu, Steamed Streaky Bacon, Bacon with Spring Bamboo Shoots, Fish with Fermented Soybean, Braised Tofu with Shrimp, and Shrimp Roe and Steamed Pork with Rice in Lotus Leaves.

After the Southern Song dynasty decided on Hangzhou as its capital, many skilled chefs from the north flocked to Hangzhou, established and developed Zhejiang cuisine, consisting of Hangzhou cuisine, Ningbo cuisine and Shaoxing cuisine, as one of the eight famous cuisines of China. Hangzhou cuisine found its own style by assimilating the essence of other regional cuisines. It is also called the "mystery cuisine," as it is difficult to discern its origins. It boasts 36 specialty dishes, including Beggar's Chicken, West Lake Fish in Sweet and Sour Sauce, Shelled Shrimp flavored with Dragon Well Tea—all as refreshing and exquisite as the West Lake itself.

Lou Wai Lou Restaurant
lou wai lou
楼外楼

With a history of more than a hundred years, this restaurant is also known as "the best restaurant in the south of the Yangtze River." Its signature dishes cover almost all representative dishes of Hangzhou cuisine.

Beggar's Chicken

Ingredients: Yue chicken from Zhejiang, Shaoxing rice wine, West Lake lotus leave.
Taste: The whole chicken is sealed in mud and roasted for three to four hours. When it is served, the mud is stripped off and the chicken is infused with the aroma of the lotus leaves and the fragrance of the wine.

Legend: In the late Ming dynasty and the early Qing dynasty, a beggar in Changshu stole a chicken, but he had no cooking utensils, seasonings or hot water to prepare the chicken. So, he cleaned the chicken, wrapped it in mud, made a fire and roasted the chicken. Soon the mud was overflowing with a sweet aroma. When the mud was dry, he stripped it off and there was the first Beggar's Chicken.

West Lake Fish in Sweet and Sour Sauce

Ingredients: Live grass carp (the fish should not be fed for one or two days before cooking in order to clean its stomach out).
Taste: Only boiled water (no oil) and seasonings are used. The fish is cooked moderately to retain its freshness, tenderness and natural flavor. When done right, the pectoral fin of the cooked fish will stand up, and it will be tender with a slight

crab-like flavor.

Legend: In ancient times lived two brothers of the Song family, who made a living by fishing. One day, a local tyrant Zhao saw the elder brother's wife, Sister Song, and became obsessed with her beauty. So he set up a trap and murdered her husband. The younger brother brought a lawsuit to the local authorities to get revenge, only to be beaten as a result. Sister Song convinced the younger brother to flee. Before his departure, she cooked a fish from the West Lake with sugar and vinegar to help him "keep in mind the bitterness of the common people" even when he led a sweet life. Later on, the younger brother became a government official and avenged his brother's murder, but he could not find Sister Song. Then one day at a banquet, he had a fish dish that tasted exactly the same as the one his sister-in-law had cooked for him. Thanks to the dish, he finally found her—she was working in another official's kitchen.

Dongpo Pork

Ingredients: Pork.
Taste: About 2 inches in size, the cubed pork is half fatty and half lean. It tastes rich, but not greasy, and has the aroma of wine.
Legend: Su Dongpo, a famous man of letters in the Song dynasty, was well respected by the local people for his good deeds when he was the local official of Hangzhou. Knowing that he loved pork, they all brought him pork when the Spring Festival came, to express their regards. Su Dongpo wanted to share the pork with the tens of thousands of migrant workers working on the West Lake dredging project, so he asked his family to chop the pork into cubes, cook it with his secret recipe, and send it with wine to each household. His family misunderstood "sending with wine" as "cooking with wine." The result was softer and more fragrant red-cooked pork that has been popular ever since. It was hence named Dongpo Pork. On the Eve of Chinese New Year, every household cooks Dongpo Pork to remember this great man.

🏠 No.30 Gushan Road, Xihu District, Hangzhou
¥ 0571-87969682 87969023

Shan Wai Shan Restaurant
shan wai shan
山外山

Located deep in the botanical garden, this century-old restaurant boasts solid craftsmanship with its many traditional Hangzhou dishes.

Fish Head Soup with Eight Delicacies

Ingredients: Fish head, netted stinkhorn mushrooms, sea cucumber, ham, chicken, prawns, bamboo shoots, shaggy mane mushrooms, sliced bamboo shoots, specially made fish balls, green vegetables.
Taste: The fish head is smooth and tender and the soup is creamy savory, and rich with its multitude of fresh ingredients.

tried their best to remove the fish bones, but failed and were executed. In the end, a chef from the streets invented the fish ball, thus solving the king's problem.

Fish Ball

Ingredients: Bighead carp from Thousand Islands Lake.
Taste: The balls are white and tender, with no fish bones.
Legend: The King Wen of Chu State (841 BC–223 BC) was very fond of fish but hated the bones. His royal chefs

🏠 No.8 Yuquan Road, Xihu District, Hangzhou
📞 0571-87986621 87995866

Zhi Wei Guan
zhi wei guan wei zhuang

知味观味庄

Located just beside the West Lake, this restaurant boasts spectacular views of the lake and the boulevard causeway. It includes six low buildings, all exquisitely decorated in different styles. Its Hangzhou style dishes are known for their classical elegance, and they are famous for their exquisite desserts.

Crab Meat Steamed in Orange

Ingredients: Live lake crab, orange.
Taste: A Southern Song dynasty dish, the poetic dish perfectly integrates the savory crab meat with the cool and fresh taste of the orange.
Legend: As recorded in a cookbook of the Southern Song dynasty, the top of the orange is cut off and cleaned of the pulp, leaving behind some of the juice. The crab meat, roe and oil are all then put into the orange cup and steamed with wine, water and vinegar in a bamboo steamer. A pinch of salt is added for seasoning at the end.

West Lake Water Shield Broth

Ingredients: West Lake water shield.
Taste: The water shield herb leaves are smooth and tender. The broth is made of fish stock, bamboo shoots, mushrooms and slivers of ham. It is a light dish typical of the region south of the Yangtze River.
Legend: It is claimed to be one of the two most savory dishes on earth (the other one is the perch of Songjiang) and was a favorite of Emperor Qianlong of the Qing dynasty during his visit to Hangzhou.

Sister Song's Fish Broth

Ingredients: Fish.
Taste: This Southern Song dynasty dish is glossy and tastes as fresh and tender as a crab meat broth.
Legend: On one of his trips to the

West Lake, Emperor Gaozong of the Southern Song dynasty met Sister Song who ran a fish broth restaurant near the Qiantang River. She entertained him with the broth and the emperor was very pleased. It soon became popular among the nobles.

No.10-12 Yanggong Causeway, West Lake District, Hangzhou
0571-87970568 87971913

Jiangnan Yi Youth Hostel
jiang nan yi
江南驿

Hot and Sour Cabbage

Ingredients: Cabbage.
Taste: It is spicy but not heavy, fragrant but not numbing. A touch of red Zhejiang vinegar makes it even more refreshing.

This unique youth hostel is known for its quiet environment and elegant style. It is very popular and a reservation is necessary.

Spiced Chicken with Sichuan Pepper Sauce

Ingredients: Chicken, Sichuan pepper.
Taste: The key to this dish is the crushed Sichuan pepper and green onion, seasoned with a pinch of salt. The juices of the onion and the fragrance of the peppers mingle and create a unique spicy aroma which perfectly sets off the natural tenderness of the chicken.

🏠 No.87 Si Yan Jing, Xiamanjuelong Road, Xihu District, Hangzhou
📞 0571-87153419 87153273

Longjing Thatched Cottage

long jing cao tang

龙井草堂

Hidden in the Longjing Village, this private farmhouse is enveloped by the surrounding beautiful scenery: the small bridge, the flowing brook, the bamboo lane and the lotus pond. All the ingredients used are purchased from nearby farms and prepared with care.

Stir-fried Tender Greens

Ingredients: Choy Sum.
Taste: 15 kg green Choy Sum produces only a small plate of this dish. As its name indicates, it is fresh and tender.

Unknown Heroes (Crucian Carp Soup)

Ingredients: Wild crucian carp.
Taste: Four wild carps (about 350–400 g each) are stewed for one hour. The fish are then discarded, and a large carp (about one kg) is then stewed in the broth until the soup is creamy and fragrant. The unknown heroes are the original four small carps which give the soup their wonderful essence.

🏠 No.399 Longjing Road, Xihu District, Hangzhou
☎ 0571-87888777

Bao Qing Business Club
bao qing hui guan
抱青会馆

With its back to the green hills and face to the West Lake, this renovated historical building is now an upscale club that still has remnants of its old-time nobility.

Goose Liver in Sake

Ingredients: Goose liver, saki.
Taste: The goose liver is marinated in the sake, giving it hints of the liquor's aroma. The liver melts in your mouth, and tastes delicate but not greasy.

Braised Tofu with Crab Roe

🏠 No.40 Beishan Road, Xihu District, Hangzhou
📞 0571-87975959

Ingredients: Tofu.
Taste: The crab roe is simmered to release its aroma. After the tofu is fried golden brown, it is added to the crab roe broth and braised until fragrant. The tofu is tender and soft, translucent like white jade and as savory as the crab.

Da Chik Mun
da zhai men
大宅门

Crab in Wine Sauce

Ingredients: Bocourt swimming crab.
Taste: The fragrant wine complements the freshness of the crab. The crab itself looks mouthwateringly shiny and is full of roe, which melts quickly in your mouth and leaves a lingering aftertaste.
Reasons of Recommendation: The main ingredient is the Bocourt swimming crab that lives where seawater and freshwater meet. The key is that the crab must be full of roe. There are strict criteria about the size, weight and freshness of the crab. Only one out of ten meets the standard. The selected crab is then cleaned and disinfected in high-alcohol liquor and marinated in a home-made wine sauce for about four days to get the hints of liquor's aroma without losing its natural flavor.

The site was home to the Temple of Zhaoxian in the Tang dynasty (AD 618–AD 907). The deserted warehouse behind this ancient building has now been redesigned into a restaurant with the grand style of an aristocratic house. The menu, the presentation of the dishes, the table cutlery, and the waiters' uniforms all exude a feeling of old wealth.

Home-made Tofu Jelly with Eight Delicacies

Ingredients: Tofu.
Taste: This tofu jelly is so smooth and fluid that it seems to slide right over the spoon. It is also so silky that it completely melts in your mouth. It is light and delicious.

No.60 Beishan Road, Xihu District, Hangzhou
0571-87992399

Yi Jia Xian Restaurant
yi jia xian
伊家鲜

Its traditional decor features the style of the region south of the Yangtze River, which is elegant and delicate. Starting off as home-style dish specialist, it has now grown into one of the top new Hangzhou-style restaurants, combining the tradition with fashion.

Maggi Hilsa Herring

Ingredients: Hilsa herring from the Fuchun River, preferably during the Dragon Boat Festival.
Taste: This is a specialty from the Yangtze River. The fish doesn't have to be scaled, as the fat beneath the scales of the Hilsa herring is rich in minerals. The fish is cooked in Huadiao rice wine and chicken broth, along with fermented rice brine, ham, shiitake mushrooms and bamboo shoots. The rice brine removes any fishy smell.

Geoduck Clam Soup

Ingredients: Geoduck clam.
Taste: This dish stews local free range chicken, goose web, ham hock, Jinhua ham, Matsutske, dried scallop, pickled vegetable, shiitake mushroom and bamboo shoots for ten hours in Longjing spring water.
Reasons of Recommendation: One day Jin Yong (1924–), a famous martial-arts novelist, was having his meal in the restaurant. The chefs prepared geoduck clam sashimi for him, but he did not like the raw and cold taste and asked to have it stir-fried. In panic, a chef mistakenly put the clam into a pot of Boiled Fish Soup with Sichuan Pickles. It turned out to be so delicious that Jin Yong wrote a couplet in praise of the dish: "It intoxicates the gourmet kung fu master and humbles the best cook."

🚄 No.221 Baochu Road, Xihu District, Hangzhou
📞 0571-87979108 87979698

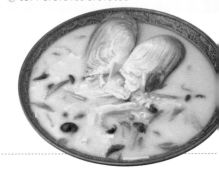

Huang Fan Er Restaurant
huang fan er
皇饭儿

A time-honored restaurant, it offers a splendid taste of the local culture.

Fish Head and Tofu Soup

Ingredients: Fish head, tofu.
Taste: The fish head is halved and fried till golden. Then it is stewed with butter, fermented bean sauce, crushed ginger, and tofu made of pure soybean. When it smells fragrant, a pinch of diced green onion is added, and it is ready to serve. The fish is both chewy and soft, the tofu savory.
Legend: One day, Emperor Qianlong went on a visit to Wushan Hill in his plain clothes and got trapped in a heavy rain, so he took his shelter in a Wang family's house. The host braised a half of a fish head with one piece of tofu and some soybean sauce for the emperor. Qianlong was so pleased that he came back to Wang's household for a second taste on his next trip to the south of the Yangtze River. He wrote three big Chinese characters *huang fan er* (the emperor's meal) for the family. Since then, the dish has become the signature dish of the Huang Fan Er restaurant.

Steamed Streaky Bacon

Ingredients: Bacon from Jinhua Shuangtouwu pigs.

Taste: It tastes soft and rich, but not greasy. The bacon is cut into big chunks (about 3–5 kg) and boiled with Jiafan rice wine, ginger and water. When it is done, it is further cut into chunks of about 100 g each and steamed in a pot.

Legend: In the old times, the detachable doors of the restaurant were its serving tables, hence the name "door meal." The steamed streaky bacon was a popular dish in this door meal, as it was delicious, served in large portions, and yet not expensive. Now it is another signature dish of the restaurant.

No.53-57 Gaoyin Street, Qinghe Fang,
Shangcheng District, Hangzhou
0571-87807768 87801068

Xin Rong Ji Restaurant
xin rong ji
新荣记

Brined Cuttlefish

Ingredients: Small cuttlefish.
Taste: It is soft and fresh.

You can enjoy a spectacular view of the lake through the restaurant's French windows. The waterside balcony is also a good place to enjoy your meal if the weather permits. The restaurant specializes in seafood and Guangdong-style cooking, focusing on the light and natural flavor of the ingredients.

Stewed Yellow Croaker

Ingredients: Yellow croaker.
Taste: The rare wild croaker tastes especially tender and fresh.

Crab Stir-fried with Ginger and Green Onion

Ingredients: Small Samoan crab.
Taste: It is tender and savory.

No.14, Yanggong Causeway, Xihu District, Hangzhou
0571-87097077 88857688

Fortune House
(Hangzhou Daily Newspaper Building Branch)
zhi fu men
指福门

Spiced Chicken with Chili Sauce

Ingredients: Free range chicken.
Taste: It is numbingly spicy, tender and fresh. The secret is the Shaanxi red ground flower pepper.

Boiled Fish Ball with Pickled Cabbage

Ingredients: Pickled cabbage, fresh fish.
Taste: These fish balls are big, chewy on the outside and soft inside.
Legend: This creation was also related to the fish-loving King Wu of Chu State. It improves on the Fuzhou Fish Ball by adding pickled cabbage to diversify the taste.

The crude red-brick walls are in sharp contrast to the exquisite heavy wood gate. The lattices extending from the walls are planted with a variety of flowers, adding a romantic touch to the restaurant.

Crystal Pork

Ingredients: Pork.
Taste: To make this dish, half a kilogram of pork is marinated with half a kilogram of sugar and other seasonings for 48 hours. It is both soft and crisp.

No.218 Tiyuchang Road, Xiacheng District, Hangzhou
0571-85052306

28 Hubin Road
hu bin 28
湖滨 28

A Chinese restaurant in the Hyatt Regency Hangzhou Hotel, it offers exquisite traditional Hangzhou cuisine and specializes in pairing wine with food.

Braised Sliced Pork in Casserole

Ingredients: Pork belly, dried bamboo shoot from Tianmu Mountain.
Taste: It is red and glossy with a rich broth. It is soft, but not greasy.
Reasons of Recommendation: It is a more delicate version of Dongpo Pork. The steamed pork is cut into cubes of about 15 cm in size and sliced into the shape of a pagoda. Each pieces still links to each other.

The original piece of pork can be as long as 30 m. The pork pagoda is then embedded with bamboo shoots, adding an elegant touch to the dish.

Shrimps with Longjing Tea

Ingredients: Fresh-water shrimp, Longjing tea.
Taste: The white, fresh shrimp are set off by the green and aromatic tea, creating a visual pleasure.
Reasons of Recommendation: In terms of ingredient selection, the shrimp should be live. They must be large but not too soft. The shrimps are squeezed out of the shells by hand to protect the membrane layer that helps retain the fresh and smooth taste. Only fresh Longjing tea picked around the Qingming Festival (falls on April 4th, 5th or 6th) is used. Pre-Qingming tea (*Mingqian* tea) picked before the festival is the best choice.

📧 Floor 1, Hyatt Regency Hangzhou, No.28 Hubin Road, Shangcheng District, Hangzhou
📞 0571-87791234

Osmanthus-flavored Sliced Lotus Roots

Ingredients: Lotus root, glutinous rice.
Taste: The crunchy and fresh lotus roots are simmered with the firm and thick glutinous rice, giving the rice the taste of the sweet, fragrant lotus. It looks reddish brown and tastes soft and slightly sticky.

West Lake No.1
xi hu yi hao
西湖一号

Located in a prime location on the West Lake, the restaurant boasts ten big lake view rooms that provide a magnificent picture of the exquisite and prospering city.

Special Mandarin Fish Soup

Ingredients: Mandarin fish.
Taste: The soup is fresh and savory, the fish tender and smooth.

Braised Delicacies from Land and Sea

Ingredients: Eight delicacies from the land (morel mushrooms, matsutake, Lion's Mane mushroom, net stinkhorn and deer lip, ect.) and eight delicacies from the sea (abalone, shark's fin, turtle rim, sea cucumber, fish maw and prawn).

Taste: The ingredients are carefully selected and the cooking procedures are extremely complicated. This dish is usually served in a jade vessel that is said to be sculpted out of volcanic rock from a plateau. In the process of cooking, the healthy minerals from the rock infiltrate into the food.

No.12 Hubin Road, Shangcheng District, Hangzhou
0571-87029988

Stop5: Guilin

Guilin

Must-go Places Introduction

General Information

Situated in the northeastern part of Guangxi Zhuang Autonomous Region on the west bank of the Lijiang River, Guilin has long enjoyed the reputation for the most fantastic natural landscapes in China. It was named after the fragrance of the osmanthus tree. As a popular Chinese saying goes, "Guilin's scenery is best among all under heaven." Its natural wonders—magical green pinnacles, crystal-clear water, picturesque rocks and intriguing caves—provide a fascinating and exciting travel experience.

Environment

Covering an area of about 4,195 sq. km, the city's municipal region is rather compact compared with other leading Chinese cities. It lies in a basin surrounded by the Yuecheng Range, Ocean Hill, Jiaqiao Range and Tianping Hill. The altitude is 140 to 160 m. The climate of Guilin is warm, moist, and moderate year round with an annual precipitation of about 1900 mm. The average temperature year round is 19°C. The coldest temperature occurs in January at 8°C and the hottest occurs in July at 28°C. The best time to travel here is between April and October.

Places of Interest

The Two-river and Four-lake Water System coils the small city, which recreates the flourishing scenery of the Song dynasty. There are many complete karsts, large soaring limestone structures, which form part of the captivating landscape in this area. The primary attractions can be summed up as "Three hills, Two caves and One river" referring to Diecai, Fubo and Elephant Trunk hills, Reed Flute and Seven-star caves, and the world-renowned Lijiang River. Nearby the river is a Stone Museum that displays intriguing geological finds.

www.guilintourist.com

Lijiang River
li jiang
漓 江

a principal tributary of the River Gui, flows from Xing'an northwest of Guilin through to Yangshuo and then joins the West River after a distance of 272 mi. (437 km).

Its waters are varied. The Guilin-Yangshuo stretch is so placid that one can see the pebbles lying on the riverbed. Elsewhere, the rapids can be difficult to negotiate.

The numerous, rugged peaks on the two sides of the meandering river offer a feast to the river traveler's eye. Yuan Mei (1716–1798), the Qing poet, marveled at the swift-changing scenery and made the following observation of the river tour. "One moment, you see the green peaks floating over your head; the next they glide under your boat."

Fishermen on bamboo rafts, their lamps lit to attract shoals of fish, add to the fairyland effect of the Lijiang River and its most scenic stretch between Guilin and Yangshuo. The men use tamed cormorants to make their catches. The Lijiang River,

Reed Flute Cave

lu di yan

芦笛岩

This magnificent cavern, packed with bizarre rock formations and stalactites and stalagmites, is in the slope of Guangming Mountain, 4 mi. (6 km) north of Guilin City. It was first discovered in antiquity, and inscriptions have been found on its walls dating back at least 1000 years. But somehow, probably because of civil war, it was forgotten for some time and then rediscovered—some say the local people kept it a secret, using it as a convenient hiding place in times of war.

Reed Flute Cave measures 787 ft (240 m) across and is divided into two sections separated by a pond forming a natural barrier. The cave features a rock called the Old Scholar, named after a sage who is said to have been so enchanted by Guilin's scenery that he began a poem about it—but, unable to conjure up words adequate enough to finish it, he turned to stone.

Other rock formations take the shape of a horse, a lion, a drum or a zither—all uncannily true to life. The cave is illuminated, and visitors are able to take in an enjoyable tour that covers about 1641 ft (500 m).

Admission:

🕐 7:30~18:00 (Apr.1~Oct.31)
  8:00~17:30 (Nov.1~Mar.31)
¥ 90
✆ 0773-2695075

Fengyu Cave

feng yu yan

丰鱼岩

Located in Shanhe 68 mi. (110 km) southeast of Guilin, Fengyu Cave is a 3.3 mi. (5.3 km) long karst cave with a subterranean river 1.4 mi. (2.3 km) long. It is named after a kind of red fish in the cave river, called Feng Yu. The cave passes 9 karst peaks and has with many large chambers, the biggest of which is more than 274,480 sq. ft (25,000 sq. m).

First developed in 1994, Fengyu Cave has been a popular and revered showpiece of the Guilin area. The stalagmites in Fengyu Cave are fairly young and are growing quickly. Most of them are slender and some paper thin. One typical stalagmite, named Ding Hai Shen Zhen (Marvelous Needle) is 32 ft (9.8 m) high but only about 5.9 in. (15 cm) in diameter. The cave can be visited by a 30-minute walk through different rock formations, followed by a boat tour on the underground river.

Admission:
🕐 8:00~17:00
¥ 60
📞 0773-7128569
@ www.cnfyy.cn

Yangshuo
yang shuo
阳 朔

There is a well-known saying that goes, "The rivers and hills of Guilin are the most beautiful in China, and those of Yangshuo surpass Guilin's."

Certainly, the contrast of limestone and tropical green, and the hills and their surrounding flat paddy lands, is one scenic aspect of this karst landscape. The Lijiang River winds through the hills like a green silk ribbon. The town of Yangshuo itself, at the end of a 50-mi. (80-km) boat cruise from Guilin City, is one of the most picturesque centers of the area and is surrounded by karst peaks that resemble ancient Chinese hats, galloping horses, a paintbrush and a five-fingered hand. All this, packed into a small town area, has inspired the following Tang dynasty saying: "The town walls encircle less than two *li* of space, but all the houses are hidden among ten thousand hills."

To the north of Yangshuo lies Xingping, which is reputed to have "the best of Yangshuo's landscape." There, fishing rafts crisscrossing the Lijiang River against a dramatic backdrop of hills are a typical sight.

Admission:
℃ 0773-8822392

Elephant Trunk Hill

xiang bi shan

象鼻山

This is another imaginatively shaped outcrop at the confluence of Guilin's Yang and Lijiang Rivers, and the subject of a rather sad legend. It is said that the King of Heaven, taking a tour of southern China, brought with him an elephant that fell ill in Guilin. A local farmer nursed it back to health, and in return the elephant worked for him in the fields. The Heavenly King considered this a betrayal and put the poor creature to death. It promptly turned to stone.

Admission:

🕐 6:30~22:00 (Apr.1~Oct.31), 7:00~21:30 (Nov.1~Mar.31)

¥ 33

✆ 0773-2586602

Fubo Hill
fu bo shan
伏波山

Standing solitarily by the Lijiang River in downtown Guilin, Fubo Hill is an impressive karst outcrop, surrounded by rolling green hills and waters, caves, picturesque rocks, and gardens. A climb to the top of the hill offers visitors an extensive view of some charming scenery.

Some believe the name comes from the rock formation's interruption of the flow of the Lijiang River. As one of Guilin's most enchanting attractions, Fubo Hill's caves contain well preserved Buddhist paintings, drawings and calligraphy dating back to the Tang dynasty. The Returned

Pearl Cave (Huanzhu Dong) and Thousand Buddha Cave (Qianfo Yan) are two of the best for ancient artwork. One stalactite in Returned Pearl Cave known as the Sword-Testing Stone is worthy of mention. It nearly hangs to the ground and is said to be the place General Fubo was testing his sword.

Admission:
🕐 6:00~18:30 (Apr.1~Oct.31),
   6:30~18:00 (Nov.1~Mar.31)
¥ 15
📞 0773-2858820

Seven-star Park
qi xing gong yuan
七星公园

This park was part of the first batch of National Tour Attractions officially recognized by the China National Tourism Administration. It is also the largest and most comprehensive park in Guilin with an area of 134.7 hectare. With its long history and numerous attractions, such as Camel Hill, Natural Stone Hall, Seven-star Cave, and Crescent Pavilion, it has been a tourist highlight since the Sui (AD 581–AD 618) and Tang dynasties.

Camel Hill
(骆驼峰 *luo tuo feng*)

Camel Hill looks so remarkably like a camel that it is difficult to imagine calling it by another name. However, there is another name that has a story to go along with it. The hill is sometimes called Ewer Hill because it is also shaped like a wine ewer. At its foot, there is a spot called the Grave

It was rebuilt in 1540 during the Ming rule at the confluence of the Small East River and Lingjian River in Guilin. It is 410 ft (125 m) long, with a total of 11 arches across its entire length. A green-tiled roof provides "wind-rain" protection, but is not as dramatic as the style of the Dong ethnic minority group. To the east of the bridge stands Hibiscus Rock. The name sounds pretty, but it is actually a symbol of suffering. It bears the watermarks of many floods that have swept across the area in the past.

of Lei the Drinker—commemorating Lei Mingchun of the Ming dynasty who used to climb to the summit to drown his sorrows in wine, lamenting the collapse of the Ming.

Flower Bridge
(花桥 *hua qiao*)

Inside the park, the renowned flower Bridge is a must-see. This elegant bridge, built of rock, reflects traditional Han Chinese architecture.

Admission:
Swven-star Cave:
🕐 8:00~18:00 (Apr.1~Oct.31)
  8:00~17:30 (Nov.1~Mar.31)
¥ 60
The Rest Part of the Park:
🕐 6:00~19:30 (Apr.1~Oct.31)
  6:30~19:00 (Nov.1~Mar.31)
¥ 35
☎ 0773-5814342
  0773-5814343
  0773-5812174

Guilin

Must-try Foods Introduction

A historic and cultural city, Guilin has long been known for having "the best landscape in China." Its local food is equally tempting.

Located in the northeast of the Guangxi Zhuang Autonomous Region, Guilin is adjacent to Guangdong Province and Hunan Province. Thus, the flavor of Guilin dishes embraces both the features of Guangdong cuisine and the flair of Hunan style: the artistic presentation and light flavor of Guangdong dishes, and the sourness and spiciness of Hunan cuisine. Some Guilin dishes are more influenced by the Guangdong style, and are thus light, tender and fresh (for example: Sautéed Lijiang Shrimps, Braised Chicken with Yellow Wine, Braised Duck with Semen Gingko), while others are more influenced by Hunan cuisine, thus always hot and sour (such as Fish Stewed in Beer and Sautéed Snails).

Guilin is also home to many Chinese ethnic groups, including the Yao Nationality, Miao Nationality, Hui Nationality, etc. These have also contributed to the formation of the unique Guilin food culture. The local ethnic snacks, such as Guilin Rice Noodles, Water Chestnut Cake and *Zongzi* Stuffed with Red Bean Paste, are all well-flavored, pure and natural.

With the development of tourism, Guilin food is also growing in variety. Huaiyang cuisine, Minnan cuisine, Chaozhou Cuisine, Northeastern cuisine and Northwestern cuisine are gaining fans. Western food, Japanese and Korean set meals are also gaining ground and are very popular with the young.

In a word, Guilin cuisine is the result of a continuous overlapping of tastes and flavors from across China and beyond.

Chunji Roast Goose
chun ji shao e
椿记烧鹅

Lijiang Boat Cake

Chunji Roast Goose is a famous brand in Guilin's catering industry. It specializes in local home-style dishes.

Chunji Roast Goose

Ingredients: Goose.
Taste: A recommendable specialty in Guilin, it is natural and pure, and tastes crisp, fresh and savory. The whole set includes the red and glossy Spicy Goose Neck, the Deep-fried Boneless Goose Pastry and the simple but fragrant Goose Soup with Kung Fu Tea.

Ingredients: *Yinnuo* (a kind of organic sticky rice grown in areas where sunlight is sparse) produced in terraces in Guilin's mountainous areas.
Taste: The two sides are deep-fried until golden, and the middle is lush green, resembling the green mountains and rivers of Guilin. It is garlic-scented, and tastes savory and glutinous.
Legend: A special snack created by the boat people living on the Lijiang River and named after its creators, it is one of the various rice cakes every household makes during the Spring Festival. It was originally available only on the pleasure boats along the Lijiang River.

No.48, Huancheng Xier Road, Xiangshan District, Guilin
0773-3823218 3856150

Jinlong Zhai
(Gold Dragon Village)
jin long zhai
金龙寨

This upscale restaurant specializes in local dishes. Its decor is characteristic of the distinctive local architecture.

Quick-fried Lijiang Shrimps

Ingredients: Shrimp from the Lijiang River, Guilin Sanhua wine.

Taste: This dish is ruby red. The shrimp tastes crisp, tender, fresh, and rich but not greasy.

Reasons of Recommendation: The cool clear water from the Lijiang River produces tender and clean shrimp. It is thought that in the shrimp one can also taste the purity and sweetness of the Lijiang River.

Guilin Fish Stewed in Beer

Ingredients: Carp, skipjack, black grass carp, Mystus Guttatus and other wild fish.

Taste: An assortment of different varieties of wild fishes, it tastes extremely fresh and savory.

Braised Pork with Lipu Taro

Ingredients: Lipu Taro.
Taste: This integrates the flavors of taro and pork and results in a fragrant combination of both.

Legend: This dish originates from the traditional Guilin Braised Fish with Yellow Wine. A chef mistook beer for cooking wine by accident when stewing the fish. As a result, the fish was strongly scented and tasted even fresher and tender. It was thus named Fish Stewed in Beer.

🏠 No.6 West Jiefang Road, Xiufeng District, Guilin
📞 0773-2824983 2838829

Yueya Lou
(Crescent Restaurant)
yue ya lou
月牙楼

Built in 1959, Yueya Lou got its name from its location at the northern foot of the Yueya Mountain in the Seven-star Park. A garden vegetarian restaurant, it is renowned for its Nun Noodles and the vegetarian dishes made by nun chefs.

Nun Noodle

Ingredients: Noodle, soybean sprout, straw mushroom, shiitake mushroom, winter bamboo shoot, Guilin tofu skin, daylily, vegetarian ham, wheat gluten.

Taste: Fragrant and refreshing, it presents wonderfully in color, smell and taste and is a great choice to replace fish, meat and other greasy foods.

Legend: Created by nuns in Guilin Crescent Mountain, the recipe was handed down to the common people and became an everyday dish.

🏠 Inside the Seven-star Park in Guilin
📞 0773-5812236

Chongshan Rice Noodle Restaurant
chong shan mi fen
崇善米粉

Chongshan Rice Noodle Restaurant is one of the best-known of its kind in Guilin. The rice noodles there are said to be the most delicious in Guilin.

Guilin rice noodles are round, thin, smooth and chewy. High quality rice is ground into liquid, then filtered and kneaded into dough, then boiled and pressed into a round shape. There are many ways of cooking the noodle. The key is the broth, as it gives the noodle its flavor. Restaurants all have their own secret broth recipes, but a typical broth is usually made of pork, ox bone, Siraitia grosvenorii and different seasonings.

Seasoned Rice Noodles

Ingredients: Rice noodle, various seasoning.
Taste: These noodles are served dry. They are quick boiled, drained, and then mixed with pork or beef slices, marinated ox tripe and ox liver, and so on. Some broth, peanut oil, crisp soybeans or chili, and diced garlic

are then added. The taste, smell and presentation are all divine.

Rice Noodles with Beef Brisket

Ingredients: Rice noodle, beef brisket and spices.
Taste: These noodles are served in soup. The marinated beef brisket slices and soybeans are boiled in a small iron pot and then poured into a bowl and mixed in with the noodles. Diced green onion, MSG, pepper and sesame oil are then added.

🏠 No.45 Yiren Road, Xiufeng District, Guilin

Guilin Ren
gui lin ren
桂林人

One can experience and enjoy the popular Guilin cuisine in Guilin Ren Food Plaza. Here there are over 1000 dishes on offer, including Guilin Rice Noodles, nutritious fast food, flavored snacks, Western combos, famous specialties from every corner of China, shaved-ice and iced drinks, etc.

Guilin Sautéed Snails

Ingredients: Guilin snail from the paddy fields.
Taste: The snails are big, fresh and tasty. The dish is very appetizing—it is sautéed with Guilin sour chili, scallion, ginger and Guilin Sanhua wine.

Deep-fried Guilin Pumpkin Cake

Ingredients: Pumpkin, rice, glucose, peanut.
Taste: It is golden in color, soft and crisp with a lingering aftertaste.

No.268 Middle Zhongshan Road, Xiufeng District, Guilin
0773-2825929

Hao Da Ma Food Plaza
hao da ma mei shi xiu xian guang chang
好大妈美食休闲广场

There are local snacks from across China in self-serve style here, and Guilin local specialties are made on the spot. The French windows allow the customers to enjoy the views of bustling downtown Guilin.

Water Chestnut Cake

Ingredients: Water chestnut, rice powder.
Taste: It is crystallized, yet sweet and soft.
Reasons of Recommendation: Water chestnuts produced in Guilin are the best in China, so the cake made of Guilin water chestnuts is especially sweet, tender, smooth and refreshing.

Guilin *Zongzi* Stuffed with Red Bean Paste

Ingredients: Top-grade glutinous rice, Guilin red bean or peanut, pork

contributes the savory and sweet tastes.

Glutinous Rice Balls with Felon Herb

Ingredients: Glutinous rice powder, peanut, black sesame, dried osmanthus and white sugar.

Taste: Though small in size, these rice balls are soft, sweet and refreshing. Above all, they are not greasy and have the distinctive flavor of the sesame and the unique aroma of the wild felon herbs. They have a lingering aftertaste.

🏠 Floor 6, Weixiaotang Commercial Building, No.37 Middle Zhongshan Road, Xiufeng District, Guilin

📞 0773-2863333

belly and bacon.

Taste: The *zongzi* (pyramid-shaped dumpling made of glutinous rice wrapped in bamboo or reed leaves) are smooth but not greasy, glutinous but not dry. The local bacon

Stop6: Hong Kong

Hong Kong

Must-go Places Introduction

General Information

Situated at the southern tip of China, Hong Kong is ideally positioned at the center of rapidly developing East Asia. Described as a "barren rock" over 150 years ago, it has become an excellent financial, trading and business center and, a premier world city. Hong Kong's population was about 6.94 million in mid-2005. It is one of the most densely populated areas in the world. Hong Kong has large amount of foreign expatriates, making up about 5 percent of the total population. The top three nationalities come from the Philippines, Indonesia, and Thailand.

Environment

With a total area of 1,104 sq. km, it covers Hong Kong Island, Kowloon Peninsula just opposite of the island, and the New Territories— the more rural section of Hong Kong, which also includes 262 outlying islands. Hong Kong is an year round destination with a mild weather from the middle of September to the end of February, and a warm and humid climate for the rest of the year. About 90 percent of the rainfall occurs between April and September.

Places of Interest

There are several important attractions to catch for first-time visitors. A voyage on the fabled Star Ferry, the Peak Tram, the islands, Po Lin Monastery, Lan Kwai Fong and Repulse Bay showcase Hong Kong's unique culture that combines Eastern and Western influences.

The cuisine of Hong Kong reflects these influences. More great restaurants are here than any place on earth. They serve the national dishes of two-dozen different countries, as well as the cuisine of virtually every province in China. The reason for the superb food in Hong Kong is simple: the Cantonese are natural gourmets. The topic of food is fundamental to the people of Hong Kong. No wonder that it is called the gourmet paradise of Asia.

Hong Kong is a shopper's delight, with a vast selection of merchandise available. It is said that anything made in the world can be found here.

www.discoverhongkong.com

Hong Kong Electric Tram
xiang gang dian che
香港电车

@ www.hktramways.com

The HK Tramways is one of the oldest public transportation systems still in operation. Inaugurated in 1904, 16 years after the Peak Tram started its service in 1888, it has provided the public with the cheapest way to travel across Hong Kong Island from Kennedy Town to Sau Kei Wan, with a branch serving the Happy Valley Racecourse. Its slow ride offers travelers a safe and leisurely way to have a first-hand look at local street life and the town. There are even open-balcony trams for tourists and private hire. While most of the trams are old-styled with slide windows, new modern trams in green and white were added to the fleet in 2000, which are more comfortable than the old ones.

The Star Ferry
tian xing xiao lun
天星小轮

The Star Ferry's green-and-white boats are the oldest in the network of Hong Kong ferries. Founded in 1898, it has served as a major communication route between Hong Kong Island and Kowloon. Lovingly cared for, they also cover the shortest distance between the Central business area and the busy shopping area in Tsimshatui. While it is still commonly used as an inexpensive mode of transportation, the 10-minute Star Ferry ride offers panoramic views of the Victoria Harbor, with IFC Phase II, the Bank of China and Hong Kong and Shanghai Bank buildings and Central Plaza on the Hong Kong side, and the HK Cultural Center, the Peninsula Hotel and Regent Hotel on the Kowloon side.

@ www.starferry.com.hk

Tung Ping Chau
dong ping zhou

东坪洲

A visit to Tung Ping Chau provides a glimpse of Hong Kong that combines colorful history and remote island isolation. A tiny island in the New Territories that has been turned into a marine park, Tung Ping Chau was used long ago by smugglers to bring guns and opium from hinterland. Almost deserted today, the main village on the island still has a few families, who offer services to weekend vacationers. A hike through the pleasant parklands is a good place to spot wild orchids native to the Hong Kong area. The island's footpaths will eventually lead to each end of the island, where there are large rock outcrops. At the island's south end are two huge rocks called Drum Rock or Watchman's Tower Rock. The long thick rock is part of the layer of rock that resembles a dragon's back. At its northern end, it is called Lung Luk Shui or "dragon entering the water."

Po Lin (Precious Lotus) Monastery
bao lian chan si
宝莲禅寺

Visitors who want to explore the outer islands in Hong Kong often make the trip to Po Lin Monastery on Hong Kong's largest island, Lautau. When first built by three monks in 1906, it only had a shrine dedicated to Buddha. It was given the current name "Po Lin Monastery" in 1924, and was expanded over the years to become one of the top ten Buddhist monasteries in Hong Kong.The world's largest bronze Buddha, 100 ft (30 m) tall and weighing 275 tons, sits on the top of Muyu (wood fish) Peak across the monastery, truly an impressive sight for all who hike up the peak to the statue.

Admission:

⏱ 9:00~18:00 (Monastery)
10:00~18:00 (Big Buddha)
Vegetarian Meals Serving Hours:
11:30~17:00

✆ 0852-29855248

Horse Racing

sai ma

赛 马

@ www.hkjc.com

Hong Kong has a long horse racing tradition. Horse racing is the most popular spectator sports in this city, which has one of the biggest jockey clubs in the world. With perfect racing courses, Hong Kong was designated as the venue of the 2008 Olympic equestrian events.

Hong Kong's famous racetracks are worth a stop. The 150-year-old Happy Valley Racecourse on Hong Kong Island and the striking Sha Tin Racecourse in the New Territories, just north of the Kowloon peninsula, can be reached via a comfortable air-conditioned train from the Central District. You will not experience horse racing like this anywhere else in the world. The racing season runs from September until June.

Repulse Bay
qian shui wan
浅水湾

Sun-drenched Repulse Bay, located in the south part of Hong Kong Island, is one of the most popular beaches in Hong Kong. Its name comes from a battle where the British fleet repulsed pirates who occupied the beach as a base.

It is always packed with local swimmers and visitors in the summer. Besides aquatic activities, Repulse Bay is a luxurious residential area for dining and relaxation that provides extensive facilities. There are restaurants and barbeque sites at the back of the beach. In addition, the area is dotted with hotels, supermarkets, and cafes.

The Zhenhai Tower Park, built in the traditional Chinese style, is located near the beach. Towering twin statues of Kwun Yum and Tin Hau, both protectors of fishermen, sit in front of the park. Overlooking Repulse Bay, is the famous "building with a hole."

The clear sparkling water with temperatures ranging from 16°C to 26°C year round, and the soft and golden sands lure visitors to Repulse Bay. In addition to these, "The Repulse Bay" and "The Repulse Bay Center" are the landmarks of Repulse Bay. "The Repulse Bay" is a residential apartment that was built on a former hotel site. "The Repulse Bay Center" in front of it is a very elegant and beautiful European building. It has a few restaurants and shops, and was filmed in a popular Hong Kong movie as well. This is certainly another place to go besides the beach.

Lan Kwai Fong
lan gui fang
兰桂坊

@ www.lankwaifong.com

Lan Kwai Fong is Hong Kong's popular haunt for dining, drinking and entertainment. This district is filled with over 100 trendy and stylish restaurants, offering a range of foods from Indian and Russian to Japanese and Californian. The street Lan Kwai Fong is L-shaped and joins with D'Aguilar Street. Both streets turn 90 degrees to form a rectangle. The gleaming atmosphere also spreads throughout the surrounding neighborhoods.

Just around the corner from the city's busy Central business district, it's the perfect place for after-work drinks and dinner with friends. When it comes to nightlife, venture down Lan Kwai Fong to find yourself in the center of the city's hottest nightspots. It's fun to stroll the streets during the evenings to see the true international mix of Hong Kong's cultural cocktail.

The Peak
tai ping shan ding
太平山顶

As the highest mountain at 522 m above sea level on Hong Kong Island, the Peak was the exclusive residential area for expatriates before 1947. The more privileged early residents made it the perfect retreat from Hong Kong's summer.

Until 1881, Alexander Findlay Smith, who had worked for Scotland's Highland Railway, managed to petition the Governor for tram routes connecting the south of Murray Barracks to Victoria Gap on the Peak. From then on, the peak gained further development.

Nowadays, a regular and reliable public transportation peak tram is available. More than a century old, this funicular tram travels up the mountain by huge steel cables, and near the top it reaches a white-knuckle pitch of 45 degrees before leveling off at 1,600 ft. The Peak offers spectacular views of the city and the harbor. It attracts some seven million visitors a year, making it one of Hong Kong's top tourist destinations.

Make sure to catch the best time —an hour before dusk to have ample time to stroll around the summit before watching a hundred million city lights start to twinkle in the city below.

@ www.thepeak.com.hk

Ocean Park
hai yang gong yuan
海洋公园

As the city's most acclaimed amusement park, Ocean Park covers more than 870,000 sq. m of land on the southern side of Hong Kong Island. Over 4 million people visit the Ocean Park each year. The park's popularity earned it a spot on Forbes top ten theme park list.

The different parts of the park are connected by a 1.5-km long cable car system, as well as the world's second longest outdoor escalator. The journey walking around the park also offers breathtaking panoramic views of the southern side of Hong Kong and the South China Sea.

At the headland, the Park boasts some of its most exciting rides overlooking the sea, including the Dragon, Abyss Turbo Drop, Crazy Galleon, Ferris Wheel, Ocean Park Tower, and Flying Swing. At the lowland, visitors can experience the joy and thrill of a ride on a 22 m diameter helium balloon that will soar 100 m into the air in the Sky Fair.

Admission:
🕙 10:00~18:00
HK$ 208/Adult, HK$ 103/Child (3~11)
✆ 0852-25520291
@ www.oceanpark.com.hk

Hong Kong

Must-try Foods Introduction

Thanks to its history and its geographic location, Hong Kong has enjoyed a reputation as an international business center and food city since the 1970s. There is a great variety of food in its restaurants, including international cuisines from Japan, South Korea, Malaysia, Thailand, India, Russia, Vietnam, the U.S., France, Germany, Italy and the Middle East. Traditional cuisines from home also abound, including Shanghai cuisine, Sichuan cuisine and Guangdong cuisine. Some restaurants keep the traditional taste of the cuisines, while others adapt to the local Hong Kong people's tastes and dining habits. It is due to these very conflicts and overlaps between the East and the West, the new and the old, the traditional and the innovative, that Hong Kong has diversified its culinary culture and developed into a metropolis of food.

Although there are many cuisines in Hong Kong, Guangdong cuisine is still the favorite of Hong Kong people. Going to tea houses for snacks is the weekly family event. However, influenced by the fast food culture, the young generation and many office workers prefer Cha Chaan Teng (local-style cafés that serve quick meals). To cover the high rents, Cha Chaan Tengs try to attract customers by catering to different tastes. They provide instant noodles, wonton noodles, sandwiches, rice with different types of barbecued or roast meat, toast, porridge, stir-fried noodles, coffee, milk tea, etc. After years of evolution, these abundant, fast, delicious and economical meals have developed into the unique Cha Chaan Teng culture of Hong Kong.

In a word, the food culture of Hong Kong is colorful and varied, random but still orderly. Foreigner or Chinese, rich or poor, you can always find a place that suits your taste.

East Ocean Seafood Restaurant
dong hai hai xian jiu jia

东海海鲜酒家

Founded in 1983, it was awarded "Best Restaurant in Hong Kong" by the *New York Times* and *Wall Street Journal* and recognized as "Top Restaurant in Wine and Food" by the French Senate in 2003.

Fried Colorful Coral Hind

Ingredients: Coral hind.
Taste: The fish is quick-fried with minimal seasoning. The key to its refreshing taste is cooking heat and the timing, both of which require an experienced chef.

Steamed Pork Dumplings with Crab Roe

Ingredients: Crab roe, pork, dumpling wrapper.
Taste: This restaurant's pork dumplings are bigger than usual, and filled with pork and fresh crab roe. The skin is golden yellow and paper-thin. They are juicy with the savory taste of the pork and crab.
Reasons of Recommendation: East Ocean Seafood Restaurant is one of the first restaurants that introduced Hong Kong to the pork dumpling, now a must-have in crab season.

The Dining Hall, the East Ocean Seafood Restaurant.
🏠 Floor 5, Miramar Shopping Center,No.132 Nathan Road, Tsim Sha Tsui, Kowloon, HK
📞 0852-23178889

nchai Branch
🏠 Floor 3, Harbor Center, No.25 Harbour Road, Wanchai, HK
📞 0852-28278887

Kamboat Seafood Restaurant
jin long chuan hai xian jiu jia
金龙船海鲜酒家

This restaurant has created varieties of dim sum to cater to all different tastes. It is the first restaurant to designate a wine-tasting section in all its branches.

Roast Goose

Ingredients: Goose, home-made sauce.
Taste: The goose is sliced into pieces just prior to serving. It goes perfectly with the sweet and sour sauce.
Reasons of Recommendation: Roasts, especially roast goose, are a special favorite of Hong Kong people.

The Kamboat goose is stuffed with home-made sauce and hung in a charcoal oven to roast. The resulting goose is glossy and juicy.

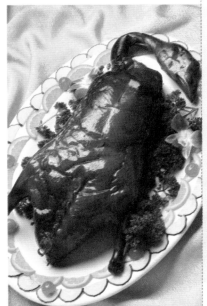

West Point Branch
🏠 No.243, Floor 2, the Westwood, No.8 Belcher's Street, West Point, HK
✆ 0852-25427448

Tsim Sha Tsui Branch
🏠 No.202, Floor 2, the Victoria Towers, No.188 Canton Road, Tsim Sha Tsui, Kowloon, HK
✆ 0852-23021708

MongKok Branch
🏠 Underground, No.113 Argyle Street, MongKok, HK
✆ 0852-27118162

Kwun Tong Branch
🏠 Floor 1, Yen Sheng Center, No.64 Hoi Yuen Road, Kwun Tong, Kowloon, HK
✆ 0852-23898939

Tsuen Wan Branch
🏠 Floor 1, Grand City Plaza, No.1 Sai Lau Kok Road, Tsuen Wan, HK
✆ 0852-24982480

Tsui Wah Restaurant
cui hua can ting
翠华餐厅

Tsui Wah Restaurant is the first upscale Cha Chaan Teng that boasts a luxurious decor. It strikes a balance between high quality food, affordable price, and the best dining environment. As a result, it attracts many office workers and foreigners. It embodies the unique culinary culture of Hong Kong. On offer are a great variety of dishes, including noodles, rice, steak, toast and porridge. It has 10 branches in Hong Kong, among which the Central branch is the best known.

Rice with Beef Brisket in Curry Sauce

Ingredients: Curry, beef brisket, rice.
Taste: The beef brisket is simmered for long hours; the result is tasty and tender.

Reasons of Recommendation: Curry dishes, including this rice set, are the signature of Tsui Wah Restaurant. Malaysian curry is very compatible with the taste preferences of people from Hong Kong and Southeast Asia. This meal set helps counteract the humidity during the sticky summer.

Hong Kong-style Bun with Butter and Condensed Milk

Ingredients: Baked bun, butter, condensed milk.
Taste: The bun is a very common item on the streets of Hong Kong. The restaurant takes the humble bun to another level by coating it with butter and then condensed milk, once the butter is fully absorbed. It is a casual touch which embodies the essence of the Cha Chaan Teng culture.

🏠 No.15-19 Wellington Street, Central, HK
✆ 0852-25256338

Daddy's Kitchen
lao die cha ju
老爹茶居

The Daddy's Kitchen is near the Tin Hau Temple. It has only 40 or so seats, but a big open kitchen. Its new branch is in an old bowling alley.

Sweet-fried French Goose Liver

Ingredients: French goose liver.
Taste: Though a small restaurant, it is true French fare. The liver looks plain, but has a great taste. It is crispy on the outside and tender inside.

Sweet-fried Scallops, Truffle and Italian Rice

Ingredients: Scallop, truffle, Italian rice.
Taste: This is a perfect merger of delicacies from the land and the sea.
Reasons of Recommendation: Chef Chan of the restaurant learned his skills with Italian rice from an Italian Michelin Two Star Chef and subsequently improved the dish with new ingredients. It offers genuine Italian taste at an affordable price.

Stir-fried Shrimp Roe Noodle with Assorted Seafood in XO Sauce

Ingredients: Shrimp, shrimp roe noodle.
Taste: An unexpected invention by the chef, this dish fuses the old and the new by combining home-made MSG and preservative-free XO sauce with an established shrimp roe noodle brand in Hong Kong.

🚪 Beside the Bowling Alley of the South China Athletic Association, Caroline Hill Road, Causeway Bay, HK
📞 0852-29795088

Dynasty Restaurant
man fu lou
满福楼

A quiet recess from the busy streets of Hong Kong, this restaurant offers a retreat into an ancient Chinese tea house with its elegant traditional décor. The French window provides a resplendent view of the hotel garden.

Shrimp Dumplings

Ingredients: Shrimp.
Taste: Known for its thin skin and quality stuffing. Only fresh shrimp is used—no other ingredients are added.
Reasons of Recommendation: This petite dumpling is bite-size, an exceptional case among the many restaurants that think larger is better.

Barbecued Pork

Ingredients: Pork tenderloin.
Taste: A very popular dish, it features Guangdong-style tenderness and richness.
Reasons of Recommendation: The tenderloin is marinated in soy sauce, wine and home-made sauce, then barbecued. The chef controls the temperature of the oven carefully and brushes the pork with honey to improve the color and taste. Only a limited amount is sold every day. Many celebrities are among its fans.

🏠 Floor 4, Renaissance Kowloon Hotel, No.22 Salisbury road, Tsim Sha Tsui, Kowloon, HK
✆ 0852-27346600

Café Deco
feng jing can ting
峰景餐厅

Located on the Peak Galleria, it has a bird's eye view of the bustling Victoria Harbor. The two levels of the restaurant are linked by a large conch-shaped staircase. The Art Deco-inspired surroundings lend an artistic flavor, but pale in comparison with the stunning views to be found looking outside the restaurant.

American-style Roast Baby Sparerib

Ingredients: Baby spare-rib, BBQ sauce.
Taste: Following American custom, this dish is served in large portions. The meat is fresh and tender. Even the bone tastes savory.

Reasons of Recommendation: Many chefs boil the rib before roasting to save time. But this restaurant chooses the traditional way: marinate the rib, roast it and brush it with home-made sauce slowly and patiently till it is done.

Soft Shell Crab with Mango Relish

Ingredients: Soft shell crab, mango, vegetables.
Taste: Each roll is bite-size, and each bite fills your mouth with the refreshing sweetness of the vegetables and mango, as well as the rich fragrance of the fried crab.
Reasons of Recommendation: In most cases, soft shell crabs are deep fried. But this restaurant takes it one step further. After the cleaned crab is deep fried and golden, it is wrapped with mango and vegetables and rolled.

🏠 Floor 1, Peak Galleria, No.118 Peak Road, Hong Kong
✆ 852-28495111

Aspasia

Although not large, Aspasia is divided into four distinctive sections with different styles. Roland Schuller, the administrative chief chef, is a Michelin Three Star Chef. After years of traveling, he returned to Hong Kong and has since made Aspasia into a renowned Italian restaurant in the city.

Tomato Water

Ingredients: Tomato, rose, vanilla, lemon juice.
Taste: As clear as water, Tomato Water can be mistaken as a cup of light Longjing tea at first glance. But the faint tomato scent betrays it.
Reasons of Recommendation: Tomato, rose, vanilla and lemon juice are boiled and then filtered and dripped, giving the Water a special, delicate fragrance.

Air-dried Tuna Roe with Macaroni and Nuts

Ingredients: Air-dried tuna roe, tuna, nuts, macaroni.
Taste: It tastes fresh and full-flavored.
Reasons of Recommendation: A masterpiece by Roland Schuller. The tuna is fried, then paired with the boiled macaroni from Italy, and arranged with the nuts on the plate. This dish, however, is mainly about the two pieces of air-dried tuna roe. Although seemingly negligible, they are the most expensive ingredients in the dish.

🏠 Floor 1, Luxe Manor, No.39 Kimberley Street, Tsim Sha Tsui, Kowloon, HK
☎ 0852-37638800

California Restaurant
jia zhou can ting
加州餐厅

Taste: The wonderful flavor of the salmon is perfectly presented.
Reasons of Recommendation: Chefs in California love creating new dishes. This one is made by slightly over-browning both sides of the salmon fillet, then pairing it with wild mushrooms and a mild sweet and sour sauce.

American Lemon Cheese Cake

Ingredients: Cheese, cranberry.
Taste: American lemon cheese cake is always one of the more popular desserts in an American restaurant. The cake is fragrant with the strong aromatic cheese and the refreshing cranberry and lemon.

Among the numerous restaurants and bars in Lan Kwai Fong, the California Restaurant has always been the flagship restaurant of Lan Kwai Fong. Guests can not only enjoy mellow wine and delicious food—they can also find remnants of *Chung King Express*, the film directed by Wong Kar Wai. Great music is played after 10:30 p.m. on Friday and Saturday nights when the restaurant turns into one of the famous discos of Hong Kong.

Salmon Filet with Sauce

Ingredients: Salmon filet, wild mushroom.

🏠 Basement No.24-26, Lan Kwai Fong, Central, HK
📞 0852-25211345

Lux Bar and Restaurant

with wine. It helps to stimulate your appetite.

Tuna with Spanish Rice

Ingredients: Tuna, vegetables, Spanish rice.
Taste: Plump tuna is cut into cubes and pan-fried, then matched with colorful vegetables and Spanish rice. It is low in calories, thus is both healthy and a treat to the eyes. It goes well with liquor and beer.

This is an entertainment restaurant that functions as a Continental-style restaurant as well as a bar and a disco. Many young professionals enjoy their evenings here: first a happy hour, then a lavish dinner and a dancing binge.

Smoked Duck Salad

Ingredients: Fresh and tender duck, vegetables, salad dressing.
Taste: A combination of fried tender duck, a slightly sweet sauce, and vegetables, this dish is colorful, fragrant and sweet. It can be served as an appetizer, or as a main course

Basement of California Building, No.30-32 D'Aguilar Street, Central, HK
0852-28689538

Sevva Restaurant
ming ren can ting
名人餐厅

This restaurant was founded by Guo Zhiyi, a Hong Kong celebrity. Since its opening, it has been a gathering place for many magnates and celebrities in Hong Kong. Located on the top floor of Prince's Building in the heart of the Central district, it overlooks the bustling Central and Victoria Harbor. The interior is chic and elegant, with vaulted ceilings, an elegant grand piano and several 20th century works of art from London Art Galleries. Most dishes are the owner's own creations, inspired by his personal experiences and travels. Such include the Rice in Soup as made by his mum, local snacks he encountered on his travels, and cakes and cookies from his friends' recipes. Thus, the resulting dishes are a fusion of local Chinese flavor, haute European and Western flavors and the true Hong Kong.

Rice in Soup

Ingredients: Rice, chicken broth, shredded chicken, shiitake mushroom, sliced abalone.

Taste: Summer in Hong Kong is humid and not conducive to the appetite. Rice in Soup is a good choice at this time of the year.

Reasons of Recommendation: Rice in Soup in Sevva is different from that one will find in other restaurants in that it was inspired by the mother of Bonnie, the restaurant's principal. The rice in soup made by his mother brought him a lot of wonderful memories in childhood. In order to make his guests feel at home, Bonnie improved the recipe of this love-filled dish, and made it a course in the menu.

Assorted Desserts

Ingredients: Various desserts, cakes and jellies.

Taste: The desserts here may excite ladies the most due to the variety of delicate desserts and jellies.

Reasons of Recommendation: Every cake and dessert made in Miss B's Cake Corner in Sevva is a result of the owner's travels in Europe and America, and therefore very European Continental.

🏠 Floor 25, Prince's Building, No.10 Chater Road, Central, HK
✆ 0852-25371388

The Lane Bar and Restaurant

This is a small, luxurious European seafood restaurant. At the gate are two fish tanks containing Boston lobsters and oysters from around the world. Dennies, the chief chef, has over ten years of cooking experience. His views on taste-matching are very original and he likes to bring out the flavor of the ingredients in a very sophisticated way.

Assorted Cold Seafood

Ingredients: Oyster, scallop, cherrystone clam, mussel, prawn, whelk.

Taste: All the ingredients are fresh. The French Belon oysters have a strong oyster flavor with a slightly metallic scent. The cherrystone clams are fresh and delicious. They can be swallowed directly with a dash of lemon juice or tomato juice. The original flavor is still very detectable.

Boston Lobster Soup

Ingredients: Boston lobster.
Taste: The soup is fragrant and smooth.
Reasons of Recommendation: This soup fully showcases Chef Dennies' pursuit for perfection. He sautés one-quarter of a lobster with tomatoes, vegetables and onions, then adds Cognac to bring the flavor up a notch. Stewed fish broth is its soup, and the lobster pincers are thrown in to fine tune the look.

🏠 Basement C, Camel Paint Center, 1 Hing Yip Street Kwun Tong, Kowloon, HK
✆ 0852-31022302

The Steak House

This 20-year old restaurant is the only BBQ and salad bar in Hong Kong. Their specialties include different cuts of top-rate grilled Australian Wagyu, such as Grade 8 Grilled Beef Rib Steak and Grades 9–12 Grilled Beef Rib-eye Steak.

Grade 8 Grilled Australian Wagyu Beef Rib-eye Steak

Ingredients: Australian Wagyu.
Taste: The freshness and tenderness of this superb Australian beef is enhanced by perfect grilling.
Reasons of Recommendation:

Before the main course is served, the waiter will bring 10 sharp knives on a black leather tray. He will introduce each knife and help the guests to choose the best one. The steak is accompanied with 12 home-made mustard jams, eight home-made sauces, eight precious natural sea salts from all over the world and 12 side dishes. The eight precious sea salts are: Alaea Hawaiian Sea Salt, Ittica d'or Sicilian Sea Salt, Cyrus Flake Salt, Murray River Pink Salt from Australia, Peruvian Pink Salt, Himilayan Pink Salt, Fumee de Sel Chardonnay Oak Smoked Fleur De Sel by Le Tresor, and

American Super-size Dessert

Ingredients: Flour, milk, chocolate powder.

Taste: Every one weighs 1.5 pounds on average, enough for two or three people to share. It is one of the specialty desserts of the restaurant due to its great taste and rich, pure chocolate flavor.

Sele Gris Coarse de Guerande. They go well with different foods and bring out the true flavors. Above all, they are very healthy.

🏠 Lobby Basement, Intercontinental Hong
   Kong, 18 Salibury Road, Kowloon, HK
📞 0852-23132323

Appendix

A Note on Chinese Cuisine

It is said that the Chinese culture is a culture of food. Chinese food is an integral part of Chinese culture, and is a must-have on any journey one takes in this nation known for its culinary delights.

Because of the wide variations in climate, natural products and customs across geographical regions, different parts of China boast cuisines of unique flavors. The ancients categorized them into eight cuisines: Lu (Shandong), Chuan (Sichuan), Yue (Guangdong), Min (Fujian), Su (Jiangsu), Zhe (Zhejiang), Xiang (Hunan) and Hui (Anhui). Su and Zhe cuisines are thought of as the comely and graceful beauties of the south, while Lu and Hui (also known as Wan) are the crude and simple men of the north; Yue and Min as dainty and refined nobles, while Chuan and Xiang are the talented scholars with rich and colorful skills.

Recent years are seeing a convergence of these eight traditional cuisines, with Huaiyang (a combination of Su and Zhe), Yue, Chuan and Lu gaining popularity

and becoming the most well-known. At the same time, many luxurious restaurants are integrating Western cooking into their dishes, with "fusion" becoming the latest fashion in Chinese cookery.

Yue cuisine has dominated the Chinese kitchen since the 1980s and is now conquering the world's stomach. There are a number of Yue cuisine restaurants in New York alone. This cuisine is known for its variety of ingredients, dishes of all shapes and colors, as well as for its innovative cooking techniques. Fresh and savory, Yue cuisine is light in summer and autumn, and richer in winter. It is full of nuances of the five senses (fragrant, soft, pungent, mellow and rich) and six tastes (sour, sweet, bitter, salty, spicy and savory) and specializes in frying, deep-frying, braising, stewing and dry-frying. The dishes are rich in color, and taste smooth but not greasy.

The Huaiyang cuisine that has attracted a lot of attention in recent years has behind it a culture bigger than the cuisine itself. Expanding on Su and Zhe cuisines, it is rich without compromising clarity; the flavors are fragrant, savory and soft. Its soup is thick but not greasy, mild and salty with a little sweetness. Its typical cooking techniques include stewing, braising, simmering and frying. Yangzhou dishes are light and delicate, with a focus on the main ingredient and exquisite cutwork. Suzhou dishes are on the sweeter side, and focus on harmony of colors. Nanjing and Zhenjiang dishes, on the other hand, are mild and feature exquisite and delicate shaping.

Lu cuisine, the acknowledged representative of the northern cuisines since the Song dynasty (AD 960–1279), was the main cuisine of the royals during the Ming (1368–1644) and Qing (1644–1911) Dynasties. Today's Lu cuisine has evolved from dishes from Ji'nan and Jiaodong, and embodies refreshing fragrance, tenderness and purity in taste. Its best soups are the savory clear soups, and the creamy soups which are milky and rich. The most renowned Lu dish today is not the classic "nine-twist pig intestine," but rather the fruit-wood roast duck from Beijing. This traditional roast duck is going healthy though—it is now low-fat and low-grease. Its meat is also used as the ingredient for several nutritional dishes.

Sichuan cuisine is popular across the world now. Chengdu and Chongqing dishes are most typical of the traditional Sichuan cuisine, with an emphasis on careful selection of ingredients, as well as harmony of colors. The tastes include sour, sweet, numbing and spicy, and the dishes are usually oily with bold flavor. Flavor is key to this cuisine. The must-haves are chili, pepper and Sichuan peppercorns (known locally as flower pepper) as well as fresh ginger. Its rich flavors, especially its spicy, sour and numbing tastes, have secured it a unique position in the Chinese culinary world, and given it the reputation "one dish, one taste; hundreds of dishes, hundreds of tastes." Sichuan chefs excel at combining flavors to make rich stock replete with layers of salty, sweet, numbing, spicy and sour tastes.

Copyright © 2010 Shanghai Press & Publishing Development Company

The Reader's Digest Association, Inc., is the authorized publisher of the English-language edition outside China.

All rights reserved. Unauthorized reproduction, in any manner, is prohibited.

Readerís Digest is a registered trademark of The Reader's Digest Association, Inc.

FOR SHANGHAI PRESS & PUBLISHING DEVELOPMENT COMPANY
Managing Directors: Wang Youbu, Xu Naiqing
Editorial Director: Wu Ying
Editors: Ye Jiasheng, Anna Nguyen
Editorial Assistant: Li Mengyao

Text and Photographs by Sun Qinqin, Zhu Ying, Tao Yu, Tang Mingjun, Wu Renzhang, Qin Shengzhong, Quanjing, Phototime, 8danyuan
Translation by Hu Lingque, Amber Scorah

Cover Design: Wang Wei
Interior Design: Yuan Yinchang, Li Jing, Hu Bin, Xia Wei

Library of Congress Cataloging-in-Publication Data

A journey through China: exploring major sites and cuisine in 10 days.
    p. cm.
ISBN 978-1-60652-122-9
1. China–Guidebooks. 2. China–History, Local. 3. Historic sites–China–Guidebooks. 4. Historic buildings–China–Guidebooks. 5. Restaurants–China–Guidebooks. I. Reader's Digest Association.
DS705.J68 2009
915.104'6–dc22
                    2009034380

FOR READER'S DIGEST
Executive Editor, Trade Publishing: Dolores York

THE READER'S DIGEST ASSOCIATION, INC.
President and Chief Executive Officer: Mary Berner
President of Asia Pacific: Paul Heath
President and Publisher, U.S. Trade Publishing: Harold Clarke

Printed in China by Shanghai Donnelley Printing Co. Ltd.

1 3 5 7 9 10 8 6 4 2